SYMMETRY

A Design System for Quiltmakers

A Design System for Quiltmakers

Ruth B. McDowell

Illustrations by Gretchen Schwarzenbach
Editing by Harold Nadel
Technical information editing by Barbara Konzak Kuhn

Cover & book design, illustration & production co-ordination by Judy Benjamin
Meridian, P.O. Box 1887, Orinda, CA 94563

Photography by Sharon Risedorph

Library of Congress Cataloging-in-Publication Data

McDowell, Ruth B. 1945-
    Symmetry : a design system for quiltmakers / Ruth B. McDowell.
        p.   cm.
    Includes bibliographical references and index.
    ISBN 0-914881-78-7
    1. Quilting—Patterns. 2. Patchwork—Patterns. 3. Symmetry (Art)
I. Title.
TT835.M277   1994
746.9 ' 7—dc20

                              93-40036
                                 CIP

Published by C & T Publishing
P. O. Box 1456
Lafayette, California 94549

Printed in Hong Kong by Regent Publishing Services Ltd
10 9 8 7 6 5 4 3 2 1

❈ ❈ ❈

*To my daughters Leah and Emily,
and to their friends*

*Alden, Alli, Amy, Andrea,
Annie, Ashley, Ben, Brendan, Brett,
Carrie, Jack, Jessica, Jim, John, Kate,
Leslie, Lucas, Megan, Peter, Samantha,
Shawn, and Susan,*

**who have kept life from being too
placid around here lately.**

CONTENTS

■ ■ ■

INTRODUCTION

■ ■ ■

Late one evening in 1981, I was gallery-sitting at our local guild's annual quilt show. There was an older couple in the gallery, carefully examining all the quilts, the husband writing brief notes about each in his program. In the show were four of my small early herb quilts; the wife and I began talking about them. She was a gardener, too, and wanted to know if I had been to art school, or how I had begun this process of designing quilts. When I responded that I hadn't graduated from a real art school, but that I did have a degree from the Massachusetts Institute of Technology, her husband joined in. He was a professor at a Boston-area college and immediately challenged me, "Why, do you realize that you ladies have used only four of the seventeen symmetries of a plane in your quilts?" He suggested that I look up Martin Buerger's book on crystallography. Now, I had had a course in the structure of materials in my years at MIT, but I hadn't considered crystallography as a source of patchwork quilt design.

Looking into the subject further, I saw clearly what he meant. In learning about the structure of materials, especially regular materials such as crystals, you must understand all the different ways identical units such as molecules can be arranged in a regular pattern. Crystallographers have, therefore, studied and codified regular patterns in linear forms, planes, and three-dimensional arrays. American patchwork quilts are frequently composed of regular repeated blocks and can be classified in the same system; that is what the professor was doing with his notes.

Having made a set of seventeen little quilts to help me understand the system better, I discovered a number of facts which have been extremely useful, both in my own quilts and in the classes I teach in beginning design. One of the primary realizations is that many more variations are possible, if you begin your quilt design with an asymmetrical block. Many of the symmetry patterns are to be found somewhere in traditional quilts, but others apparently have never been used. This book is an outgrowth of a decade of fascination with this process, both in my own quilts and with more than a thousand students.

This book has been designed for you to use it in a number of ways. At the most simple level, you can use it as a pattern book: each of the seventeen quilts illustrated can be copied directly from the templates, directions, and yardage charts provided.

On another level, you can use it for an investigation of symmetry, to expand your vocabulary of design ideas which you can interpret in your own original quilt block designs or, indeed, in other types of surface design.

Or, you may want to use some of the illustrated blocks in other arrangements. Any of the square or rectangular blocks in Part 1 can be used in any of the symmetries in Part 1, in addition to the arrangement given in the book. Some of the blocks from Part 2 can also be used in symmetries other than the ones for which they were drawn.

I have included quilts that are very easy to piece, and ones that will challenge the most advanced sewer. While some require a multitude of templates, the sewing process is straightforward.

I have also designed the quilts to use a range of different colors and fabric choices. They may suggest possibilities for unusual fabrics that you can use in your own designing. Grainlines are not marked, but try to avoid outside bias edges.

Each of the quilts has been quilted in a different way, three by hand and fourteen by various types of machine quilting techniques. The process of selecting the quilting system to use on a finished top can be complicated. The quilts in this book will give you examples of the ways in which different types of quilting choices affect the surface of the piece.

Yardages are given for each quilt. For those that are essentially scrap quilts, or for those where I have made subtle color changes for some blocks, the yardages are given as though you were using a single set of fabrics for all the blocks. The yardages for the borders are given separately. If you intend to use some of the same block fabrics for the borders, remember to add together the block yardage and the border yardage to get the total amount you will need.

SYMMETRY IN TRADITIONAL BLOCKS

A hallmark of patchwork quilts in America is the use of a repeated block to produce an overall pattern. There are hundreds of such traditional blocks, each with one or more names, which have been used to make thousands of quilts.

Traditional patchwork blocks are almost always square in format. They are usually categorized by major design elements: four-patch, nine-patch, pinwheel, etc. Most traditional blocks have some degree of symmetry built into the block itself.

In this book, we will be looking at quilt blocks in a new way. Let's examine some traditional blocks.

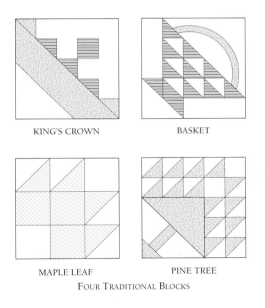

KING'S CROWN   BASKET

MAPLE LEAF   PINE TREE

FOUR TRADITIONAL BLOCKS

With each of these patterns, the traditional approach is to describe the block as the unit square in which these patterns appear. In fact, if you cut each of these square blocks in half along the diagonal, you will see that one half of the square block, a right triangle, is a mirror image of the other half of the block.

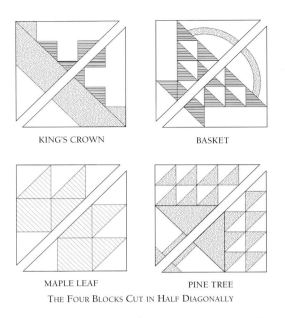

KING'S CROWN   BASKET

MAPLE LEAF   PINE TREE

THE FOUR BLOCKS CUT IN HALF DIAGONALLY

The design in one of these right triangles includes all of the elements that define the block design. One right triangle can be flipped over and the two right triangles combined to produce the traditional block. Alternatively, you can place a mirror along the diagonal edge of one triangle and see the traditional block. This diagonal edge, the hypotenuse, the edge of the mirror, is called a "mirror line" in this type of pattern. One of the right triangles is the smallest repeating unit from which the traditional block can be constructed.

Basic units from which these traditional blocks can be constructed:

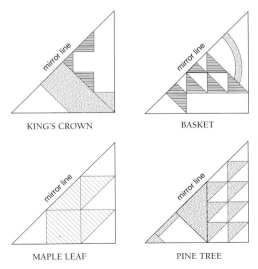

KING'S CROWN   BASKET

MAPLE LEAF   PINE TREE

BASIC CONSTRUCTION UNITS FOR THESE BLOCKS

The unit triangle is used with its mirror image to produce the traditional block; then the blocks are repeated in various regular ways to produce the pattern on the surface of the quilt.

Unit pattern for Maple Leaf:

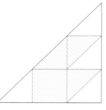

BASIC UNIT FOR MAPLE LEAF

Three traditional Maple Leaf overall arrangements:

THREE TRADITIONAL MAPLE LEAF ARRANGEMENTS

Here's another type of traditional block, commonly referred to as pinwheels.

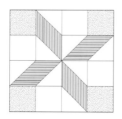

CLAY'S CHOICE

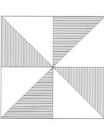

WINDMILL

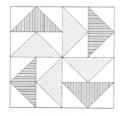

ECCENTRIC STAR

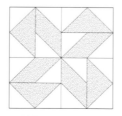

JACK-IN-THE-BOX

FOUR TRADITIONAL PINWHEEL BLOCKS

In each of these cases, the block can be cut in quarters, and each of the quarters will contain the same small design. Spinning one of these quarter units around one corner like a pinwheel will produce the design in the traditional block:

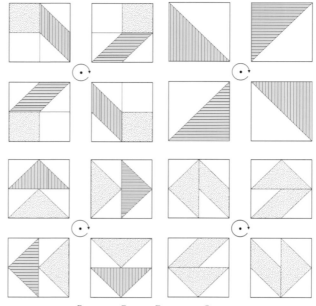

PINWHEEL BLOCKS DIVIDED IN QUARTERS

The smallest unit from which these pinwheel blocks can be made is one quarter of the traditional block.

Basic units from which these pinwheel blocks are constructed:

CLAY'S CHOICE

WINDMILL

ECCENTRIC STAR   JACK-IN-THE-BOX

BASIC UNIT FOR THESE FOUR PINWHEEL BLOCKS

Many traditional quilt blocks are arranged in a third way:

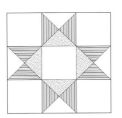

VARIABLE STAR

SKY ROCKET

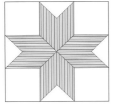

LE MOYNE STAR

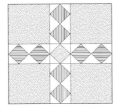

BIRD'S NEST

FOUR OTHER TRADITIONAL BLOCKS

Each of these blocks can be cut in quarters to produce smaller identical square units (each turned a quarter of a turn from the other):

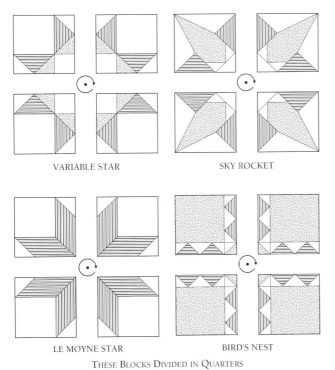

VARIABLE STAR

SKY ROCKET

LE MOYNE STAR

BIRD'S NEST

THESE BLOCKS DIVIDED IN QUARTERS

But each of these small square units can be cut in half diagonally like our first examples, and the resulting right triangles will be mirror images of each other:

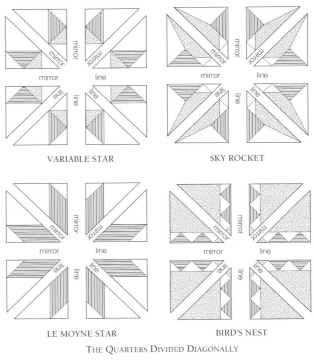

VARIABLE STAR

SKY ROCKET

LE MOYNE STAR

BIRD'S NEST

THE QUARTERS DIVIDED DIAGONALLY

Placing a mirror along the two interior edges of the unit triangle will produce the traditional block. So, the smallest unit from which this type of block can be made is this small right triangle. It has mirror lines along two edges. Eight of these unit triangles, four plain and four mirrored or reversed, will make up the traditional block.

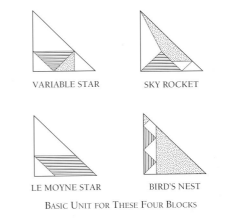

VARIABLE STAR

SKY ROCKET

LE MOYNE STAR

BIRD'S NEST

BASIC UNIT FOR THESE FOUR BLOCKS

A few traditional blocks contain no repeated elements and cannot be subdivided in this way. These traditional blocks were designed without any built-in symmetry. They are asymmetrical.

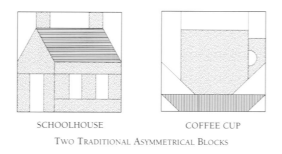

SCHOOLHOUSE   COFFEE CUP

TWO TRADITIONAL ASYMMETRICAL BLOCKS

In designing original blocks, you can create many more overall patterns if the original block (unit) is asymmetric in this way. The quilts in this book will demonstrate that. In addition to the square format of most traditional blocks, other quilt block shapes are possible, as we shall also see.

TYPES OF SYMMETRY

There are many ways of arranging the traditional blocks in an overall symmetrical pattern. Here, for instance, are three different overall patterns that can be made from the traditional Pine Tree block:

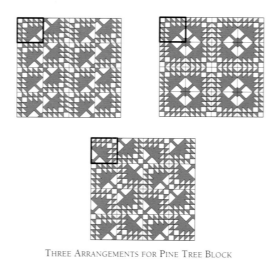

THREE ARRANGEMENTS FOR PINE TREE BLOCK

In investigating symmetry in this book, we will be looking at two elements: the asymmetric "unit" from which the design or "block" is made, and the overall symmetric pattern in which the "units" are placed.

People have used repeated patterns for thousands of years to produce all kinds of designs. Scientists have studied repeated patterns in their attempts to understand how things are put together. They have looked at regular pattern very closely in the study of crystallography and developed a system of describing symmetry in pattern. That kind of study can be applied to the study of pattern in quilts as well.

A discussion of the regular ways that units can be repeated to form an overall pattern leads to an initial discussion of the four types of symmetry. These are:

Mirror symmetry

We saw this in the first type of quilt blocks that we looked at. One half of each of these traditional blocks is the mirrored or reversed image of the other half. This type of symmetry occurs frequently in nature, as in the two wings of a butterfly or the two halves of a face, or in a pair of hands. These patterns can be produced by placing a mirror along the center; each contains a "mirror line":

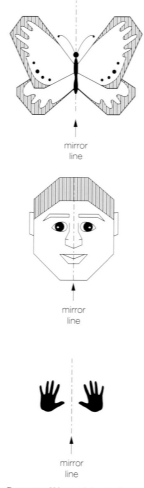

PATTERNS WITH A MIRROR LINE

Rotational symmetry

This is the pinwheel pattern found in the second type of traditional blocks we looked at. A unit is spun around a point to produce a rotated pattern:

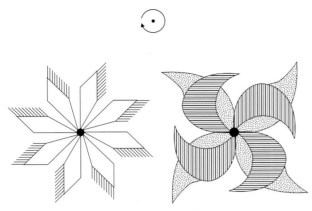

PINWHEEL OR ROTATIONAL PATTERNS

Translational symmetry

Here, each unit is repeated one after the other, all facing the same way, like a sheet of postage stamps. The unit is slid right or left, up or down, but not mirrored or rotated:

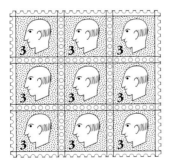

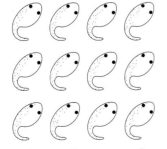

POSTAGE STAMP OR TRANSLATIONAL SYMMETRY

Glide symmetry

I have never found this fourth type of symmetry in a traditional quilt. It is a combination of both translation and mirroring, but the resulting pattern contains no mirror lines. It cannot be produced by placing a mirror next to the original unit:

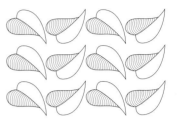

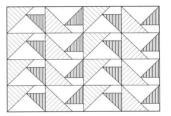

PATTERNS WITH GLIDE SYMMETRY

Crystallographers, in studying plane (flat) regular repetitions, have developed a set of seventeen patterns using these basic types of symmetries. It is these seventeen symmetries of the plane that we will be looking at as overall arrangements of blocks in this book, to explore their implications for new and exciting quilt designs.

THE SEVENTEEN SYMMETRIES OF A PLANE

I have divided the seventeen symmetries into two separate parts of this book. The first eleven are easily laid out using square or rectangular blocks. They will be described in Part 1. The remaining six symmetries are most easily done with blocks of other shapes and constitute Part 2.

In order to explain the twists and turns and mirrors that make up symmetrical repeated patterns, crystallographers have devised a number of notation systems. I have found it convenient to use handprints as symbols. A handprint is an asymmetric unit with a thumb on one side. A right handprint is a mirror image of a left handprint. Each of the seventeen symmetries will include a group of handprints that will serve to depict the symmetry.

For the eleven symmetries of Part 1, I have also included a sketch of the possible patterns using the Clay's Choice "unit" block, so that you can compare one symmetry to another and begin to understand the many more overall patterns possible by beginning your designing with an asymmetric block.

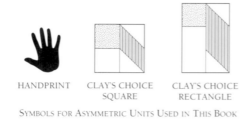

HANDPRINT   CLAY'S CHOICE   CLAY'S CHOICE
SQUARE   RECTANGLE

SYMBOLS FOR ASYMMETRIC UNITS USED IN THIS BOOK

A LESSON PLAN FOR AN INDIVIDUAL OR A GROUP

This book can be a valuable resource to introduce you to the process of making your own original designs. You can work on your own, or you may want to investigate symmetry designing with a group of friends or in a formal classroom set-up with an experienced teacher. In a group or classroom, you will have the advantage of sharing your discoveries with others in the learning process, and of seeing many types of designs worked on simultaneously.

An interesting way to explore the first eleven symmetries is to design an original block. When teaching a workshop on this material, I begin by having each student draw a 2" square (or 10 cm square), or a rectangle of that approximate size on graph paper. Within the

square (or rectangle), each student makes a simple asymmetric design of 5 to 8 pieces, with straight lines, curves, or both. The design need not be complex; it is the process we are investigating. Check carefully to make sure your design is asymmetric. (Blocks that mirror symmetrically along a diagonal line are the ones in which the symmetry is most often missed. Check carefully for this.)

Occasionally a student has become so accustomed to the symmetry built into most traditional quilt blocks that she finds it almost impossible to design an asymmetric one. Should that be a problem, there is an easy way out: Draw a 2" (10 cm) square on the graph paper. Hold your ruler high in the air, then drop it on the square. Draw a line where it lands. Repeat this process several times. I can almost assure you that you will have made yourself an asymmetric block design.

Rules are made to be broken. But, based upon years of experience, I offer a few hints. Blocks with a solid bar down one side tend to produce less exciting designs. If you have a bar, break it up or eliminate it. If you have lines drawn at odd angles, arrange them to begin and end on intersections of your graph paper: it will be easier to re-draw them in the next step of the process. (Feel free to ignore both of these suggestions.)

When your block has been designed, you will need to make a number of copies of it, all identical. Sixteen is a good minimum number to work with. You can fit sixteen 2" squares on an 8½" x 11" piece of graph paper. For rectangular or metric blocks, you may need more than one sheet.

You will also need sixteen mirror images of your original block. These can be made in a number of ways:

■ Option 1. You will be drawing your sixteen 2" square blocks, edge to edge, on the top sheet of a pad of graph paper. Before you start to draw, lift up the top sheet and the second sheet of your pad and insert a piece of carbon paper, carbon side up, under the second sheet. As you draw the sixteen blocks on the top sheet, the sixteen mirror blocks will come out on the back of the second sheet. Number the corners of each block 1,2,3,4 and two of the sides A and B on each block before you rip the sheets off the pad.

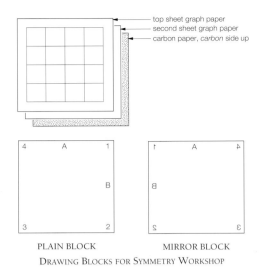

top sheet graph paper
second sheet graph paper
carbon paper, *carbon* side up

PLAIN BLOCK   MIRROR BLOCK

DRAWING BLOCKS FOR SYMMETRY WORKSHOP

If your paper is not on a pad, you should pin, staple, or tape two sheets together so they don't slip. Bear down hard so the carbon copies are dark.

■ Option 2. Draw sixteen blocks, edge to edge, on a piece of graph paper with a fine-line permanent marker. Number the corners of each block 1,2,3,4 and two sides A and B on each block. The marker will bleed through the sheet enough that you can turn the sheet over and trace over the lines to make mirror blocks. On a copy machine, copy both sides of the sheet, onto card stock if possible.

■ Option 3. Draw sixteen blocks as in option 2, but with pencil. Turn the sheet over and place it against a light box or a window to trace over the lines of the mirror blocks. Number the corners of each block 1,2,3,4 and two sides A and B. On a copy machine, copy both sides of the sheet, onto card stock if possible.

■ Option 4. Draw sixteen blocks, edge to edge, on one sheet. Number the corners of each block 1,2,3,4 and two sides A and B. Have an acetate (clear plastic sheet) made on a copy machine. Have two copies made, on card stock if possible, with the acetate first one surface up, then the other surface up.

■ Option 5. Draw one block. Number the corners of each block 1,2,3,4 and two sides A and B. Have an acetate made on a copy machine. Make sixteen copies of the acetate with one side up, then sixteen with the other side up. In a group or classroom, you may be able to tape several people's blocks together and copy them all at once.

■ Option 6. Use a computer to generate your copies

and mirror blocks with the number and letters in place.

If your blocks are on paper rather than card stock, glue the sheets onto lightweight cardboard or a file folder to give them some stiffness; they will be easier to handle.

In all cases, make sure the corners of each block are numbered and two sides lettered before the copies are made. The lettering on the mirror blocks will be reversed, but in the proper location.

Now, cut the blocks apart to make sixteen cards of plain blocks and sixteen cards of mirror blocks. With these two sets of cards, you will be able to lay out each of the first eleven symmetries by matching the numbers 1,2,3,4 and A and B with the diagrams.

With access to a copier, you may want to make enough duplicates of your original blocks to paste up all the patterns in Part 1 so that you will have a permanent record of your own designs.

2" Square Blocks
14 sheets of 16 plain blocks (216 blocks needed)
9 sheets of 16 mirror blocks (136 blocks needed)

Rectangular Blocks
302 total plain blocks
200 total mirror blocks

Now you are ready to proceed with your investigation of symmetry using your own design for a 2" paper block. If you are working in a group, you will be able to share the patterns that develop with your neighbors. You will all learn more about the design process as you look at the transformations of a number of different blocks. Remember, you are studying a process. The blocks you have designed are deliberately rough and simple. Some of them will look very interesting in particular symmetries, others in other symmetries. You may want to design a more elaborate block when you have finished with the exercise, based on the experience you have gained.

I have my workshop students use the simple line patterns as you have drawn. Other teachers have students shade blocks with grays, or color them with markers or snips of fabric. I believe that more possibilities for design will occur to you if you have not locked yourself into a particular color scheme at the beginning.

The paper blocks you have made will be used to lay out the symmetries in each of the chapters of Part 1. Careful diagrams in each chapter will guide you through the process. Let's get started!

PartOne

ELEVEN SYMMETRIES FOR SQUARE
& RECTANGULAR BLOCKS

Let's begin now to look at the regular arrangements of block units — the symmetries. For each of the first eleven symmetries, I have designed an original asymmetrical block in a square or rectangular format. As we will discuss later, we can also use each of these blocks in the other ten first symmetries to make other quilts. In the years in which I have been working with this system of designing, I have become aware that certain symmetries lend themselves to certain types of designs. In my workshops, each student creates an original block design with which to work. In helping my students with their blocks, I have found that one symmetry (P4) produces lively aster-like flowers. Another (P2MG) often appears to look like schools of fish swimming in opposing directions. I've taken advantage of these tendencies in designing blocks for this book.

However, any of the square or rectangular blocks in Part 1 can be used in any of the eleven symmetries of Part 1, in each case producing very different designs. The P4 block will not make asters in all of the symmetries, nor P2MG make schools of fish, but the resulting graphics will be interesting in other ways.

Crystallographers have developed a method of notation to describe the symmetries based on a few simple concepts:

- P = plane: The pattern described is on a flat (plane) two-dimensional surface — for our uses, a quilt.

- M = mirror: There will be a mirror line or lines such as we have seen in looking at the preceding traditional blocks.

- G = glide: There will be both plain and reflected (mirror image) units, but no mirror lines. The symmetry is formed by simultaneously sliding and flipping the units. I have never found it in a traditional quilt, but have found that glide symmetry makes some wonderful designs. (This will be explained in detail further on.)

- C = centered lattice: This is a symmetry with an off-set arrangement rather than stacked elements. We will work with two such symmetries.

- 2,3,4,6 = number of repeated units in a full 360° rotation: Again this will be demonstrated as we get to them.

Now, *relax*. These may seem complicated at first but, with a little practice, you will find them a useful way to describe the symmetries. As we work through the process, you will pick up these terms by osmosis. Trust me.

In the sketched notation that accompanies each quilt, the mirrored blocks are labeled with a capital R (Reversed). If you have made your own paper blocks with which to try the symmetries, you may want to label your mirrored blocks with an R as well. Mirror lines will be indicated with an m⟶.

In order that we be consistent, we will define "row" to mean a horizontal line, and "column" to mean a vertical line.

If I were approaching the quilts that I will be making strictly to demonstrate symmetry, I would choose one color scheme for each block and keep to that color scheme absolutely in all of the blocks of the quilt. Symmetry would require that all blocks in a quilt be colored the same.

However, the artist in me rebels at so much restriction of my color choices. I have been freer with my choice of colors than strict adherence to symmetry patterns would demand. In the interest of making a more interesting surface design, I have varied the colors in some of the blocks in some of the quilts, sometimes in an orderly way and sometimes randomly. In Viola and Musical Notation, each block in the quilt is colored exactly the same. In Painted Daisies, the background pieces and centers are the same colors in each of the sixty-four blocks, but the flower petals are colored differently in groups of four. I've painted the daisies sixteen different colors in the overall quilt. In the Poppies quilt I've used darker reds in sixteen of the poppy blocks to add variety to the center of the quilt, then created a border by piecing parts of the poppy blocks in purples. In Deco Moon, half of the blocks are slightly lighter fabric choices than the others, empha-sizing the horizontal rows. With Spinning Rings, the blocks form colored borders around the central sixteen blocks.

In all of my designing, the regularity of repeat is there to be used or not as I, the artist, choose. Since the focus of this book is on your learning the symmetry patterns and understanding what an asymmetrical block can do for you, I have chosen to keep those parts of each quilt regular. No blocks are turned out of the position the symmetry requires. But I also use the quilts to give you lots of ideas and suggestions about color and fabric choices that may help you make more interesting quilts and quilt borders.

As the artist, you make the choices!

Viola

■ ■ ■

A sheet of postage stamps describes this symmetry. All of the blocks are oriented in the same direction. No mirror blocks are used. The simplest symmetry arrangement, this is frequently used in traditional quilts.

For this book, I have designed a block with a single viola (or pansy) blossom. If you make the two upper petals purple, and the three lower ones yellow, you will have Johnny-jump-ups. Or choose the colors from a flat of mixed pansies and make each blossom a different color: blues, violets, purples, apricot, yellow, ruby red, and white for a Spring garden. Large-scale brushstroke prints might be cut up to make the dark zones seen at the center of some pansies.

For the Viola quilt illustrated, you will need nine Viola blocks, each 9" square. The Katsura Leaf block in Chapter 8 is also made in a 9" square. I couldn't resist using the Katsura Leaf, this time in greens, to border the violas: artistic impulses sometimes overrule orderly presentation. To give the border some motion, I used eight plain Katsura blocks and four reversed Katsura blocks, with simple corner blocks to finish. A slightly different border could be made with twelve plain Katsura blocks plus corner blocks, or sixteen plain Katsura blocks without the addition of corner blocks.

These elaborate borders, of course, may be more than is really necessary. Much simpler borders would work as well — perhaps strips and corner squares. Try various versions, pinning up folded strips of possible bordering fabrics next to your pieced Viola blocks. Step back and carefully consider which choices enhance the center.

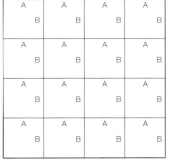

SYMMETRY NOTATION FOR P1

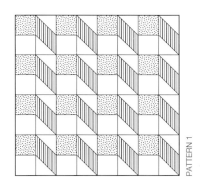

PATTERN 1

TO MAKE THE QUILT ILLUSTRATED
Finished size: 45½" x 45½" (115 x 115 cm)
9 Viola Blocks: 9" x 9"

	TEMPLATE								
Color	1	2	3	3R	4	5	5R	6	7
Yellow	-	-	-	-	-	9	-	-	9
Plaid	-	-	-	-	-	-	9	-	-
Purple	-	9	-	-	-	-	-	9	-
Background	72	27	9	9	9	-	-	-	-
Yellow-green	9	-	-	-	-	-	-	-	-

	TEMPLATE				
Color	8	9	10	Yardage	Meters
Yellow	-	9	9	⅜	0.375
Plaid	-	-	-	⅛	0.125
Purple	9	-	-	¼	0.25
Background	-	-	-	¾	0.75
Yellow-green	-	-	-	⅛	0.125

Border

Using Katsura Leaf block from Chapter 8: 8 plain blocks, 4 reversed blocks, 4 corner blocks

TEMPLATES FROM CHAPTER 8 — KATSURA LEAF BLOCK							
	1	2	3	4	5	5R	6	6R
Background	12	24	12	24	8	4	12	12

	7	7R	8	8R	Yardage	Meters
Background	-	-	-	-	1¼	1.25
Green	8	4	8	4	1	1

Corner blocks

From plaid fabric, cut 4 (4½" x 4½"), from dark fabric, cut 8 (4½" x 5½") and 4 (5½" x 5½")

Plaid	⅛	0.125
Dark	¼	0.25
Backing fabric	3¾	3.75

QUILTING

Quilting on the Viola was done by machine. Free-motion quilting added veins to the viola blossoms and to the leaves in the border. Two varieties of programmed satin stitches were used in the center of each flower. The background of the Viola blocks and Leaf blocks, and the corner blocks, are stipple quilted with a small meander pattern in black thread. Cotton batting.

ASSEMBLY

Sew
- 1a to 7 to 2a to 3 to 2b
- 5 to 5R to 9 to 1b to 1c to 1d to 1e
- 1f to 6 to 4
- 2c to 8 to 1g
- 1i to 10 to 1h to 3R to 2d
- 1a,7,2a,3,2b to (5,5R,9,1b,1c,1d,1e)
- (1f,6,4) to (2c,8,1g) to (1i,10,1h,3R,2d)

Join the sub-units.

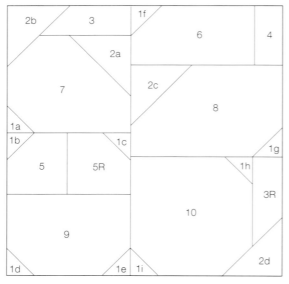

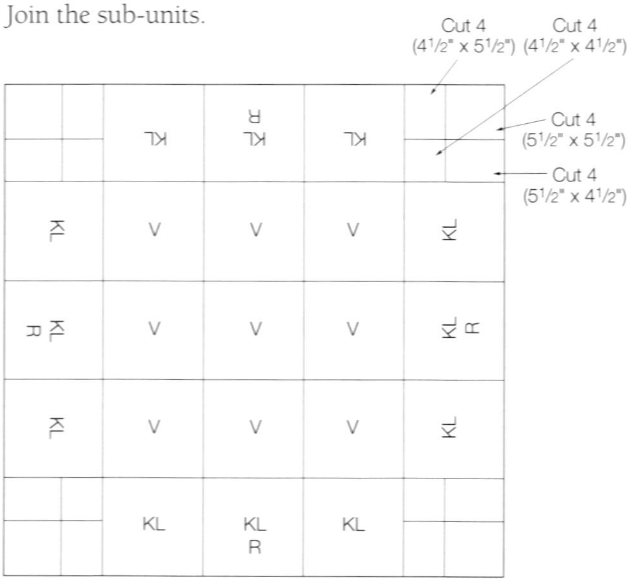

LAYOUT FOR VIOLA BLOCK

LAYOUT FOR VIOLA QUILT

MusicalNotation

■ ■ ■

Compare the diagrams for P2 with those for P1 in Chapter 1. Each block in the top row of P2 is the same as P1. In the second row, each block of P2 has been turned through 180° (upside-down).

If you have made paper blocks of your own, lay out the pattern by starting with a row of four plain blocks with Side A at the top. Underneath this, make a row of four plain blocks with Side A at the bottom. Repeat these two rows. A second pattern can be developed with the same blocks, same symmetry, by laying out the first row with Side B at the top, and the second row with Side B at the bottom.

The block I have designed for P2 is a small rectangle that is relatively easy to piece. The black spot is part of a polka-dot fabric. I cut Template 1 out of plastic and marked the location of the dot on the template. I could then see through the template and line it up accurately with the dots on the fabric. This process depends, of course, on finding a fabric with huge polka dots. With plain fabrics, the dot can be appliquéd by hand or machine onto the piece of fabric cut with Template 1 before the block is sewn together.

I find it tremendously exciting to incorporate the whole range of available fabrics in my quilts: solids and calicoes, plaids, hand dyes, medium and large scale prints, drapery fabrics, and fabrics from different eras and different parts of the world. Making a quilt from disparate parts is a visual challenge and lots of fun.

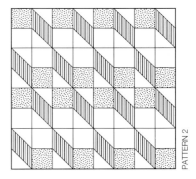

PATTERN 2

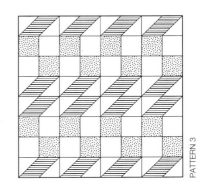

PATTERN 3

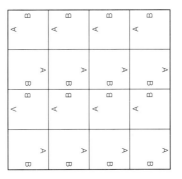

SYMMETRY NOTATION FOR **P2**

TO MAKE THE QUILT ILLUSTRATED

Finished size: 37½" x 28½" (95 x 72 cm)
36 Musical Notation Blocks: 3½" x 5"

| | TEMPLATE | | | | | | |
Color	1	2	3	4	5	Yardage	Meters
Polka Dot	36	-	-	-	-	½*	0.5*

* The yardage necessary will vary, depending on the design of the polka dots. You will need enough for 36 pieces 3" x 4".

Red	-	36	-	-	-	⅛	0.125
Black stripe	-	-	-	36	-	⅛	0.125
Black	-	-	-	-	36	¼	0.25
Green	-	36	-	-	-	⅛	0.125
Blue	-	36	-	-	-	⅛	0.125
Red print	-	-	36	-	-	⅛	0.125

Borders

Red print	½	0.5
Cut 2 (30½" x 4") for the side borders		
Cut 2 (28½" x 4") for top and bottom borders		
Backing fabric	1	1

QUILTING

The quilt is hand quilted, in the ditch around each block, along diagonal lines, and around the outside edge of the polka dots. The border is quilted along the curved lines printed on the red fabric. Polyester batting.

ASSEMBLY

Sew   2a to 3 to 1
           2b to 4 to (2a,3,1)
           2c to 5 to (2b,4,2a,3,1)

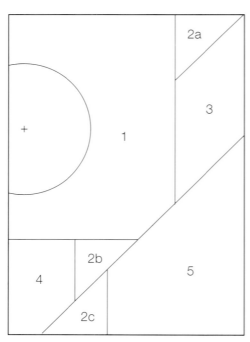

LAYOUT FOR MUSICAL NOTATION BLOCK

LAYOUT FOR MUSICAL NOTATION QUILT

PaintedDaisies

■ ■ ■

Four-way rotation, P4, makes pinwheel patterns and is common in traditional quilts. To lay out the pattern with your paper blocks, start by making a group of four blocks with Corner 1 in the center. Make three more identical groups of four and arrange them in a sixteen-block square. You will find four identical pinwheels where Corner 1's touch and another pinwheel in the center of the group of sixteen where Corner 3's touch.

Another overall pattern will develop if you begin with a group of four blocks with Corner 2 in the center. Make three more identical groups (with Corner 2's in the center) and arrange them in a sixteen-block square. You will find four identical pinwheels where Corner 2's touch and another pinwheel in the center of the group of sixteen where Corner 4's touch.

With square blocks there are two patterns possible with P4 symmetry, and the blocks fit together perfectly.

With rectangular blocks, you will need small square background blocks to fill out the surface in P4 symmetry. The dimension of the squares is the difference between the length of the two sides of the rectangle.

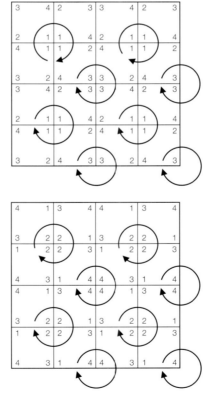

SYMMETRY NOTATION FOR P4

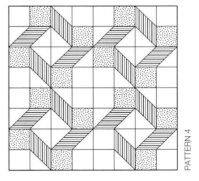

PATTERN 4

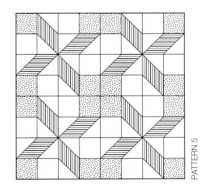

PATTERN 5

To lay out P4 symmetry with rectangular blocks, begin by making a group of four with Corner 1's in the center. Make three more identical pinwheels with Corner 1's in the center and arrange them as shown below.

You will find four pinwheels where Corner 1's touch, and another pinwheel at the center of the group of sixteen blocks, centered around a small square. There are three other P4 patterns that can be formed with rectangular blocks, as illustrated below.

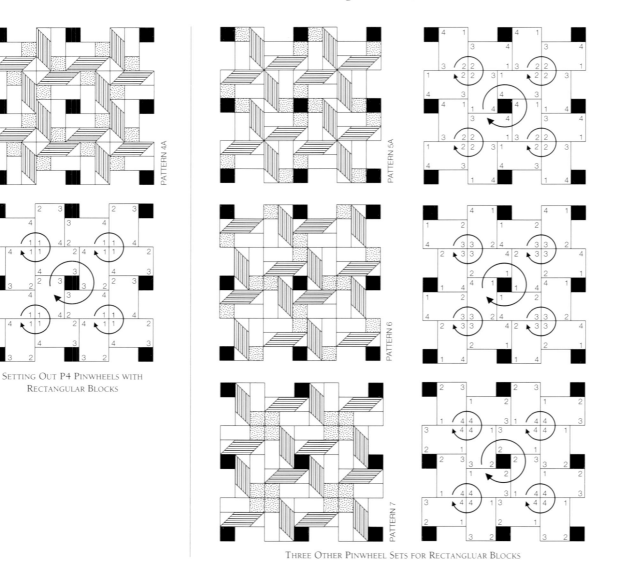

SETTING OUT P4 PINWHEELS WITH
RECTANGULAR BLOCKS

THREE OTHER PINWHEEL SETS FOR RECTANGLUAR BLOCKS

TO MAKE THE QUILT ILLUSTRATED

Finished size: 69½" x 69½" (176 x 176 cm)
64 Painted Daisy Blocks: 6" x 8"

	TEMPLATE								
Color	1	2	3	4	5	6	7	8	9
Petals	-	4x16	-	-	4x16	-	-	4x16	-
(Each flower is different: cut 4 of each petal from 16 fabrics)									
Background	64	-	64	64	-	64	64	-	64

	TEMPLATE				
Color	10	11	12	Yardage	Meters
Petals	-	-	-	¼ each of 16 fabrics	0.25 each of 16 fabrics
Background	-	-	-	1½	1.5
Yellow	64	-	-	¼	0.25
Turquoise	-	25	-	¼	0.25
Lavender	-	-	16	¼	0.25

Borders

Inner border

Leaf print   1¾   1.75

Cut 2 (4" x 58½") for top and bottom borders, cut 2 (4" x 65½") for side borders

Outer border

Blue stripe   2   2

Cut 2 (2½" x 65½") for top and bottom borders, cut 2 (2½" x 69½") for side borders

Backing fabric   4¼   4.25

I have chosen to design a rectangular block for P4 which forms a daisy-like flower when used with Corner 1 in the center of the pinwheel. I was inspired by a quilt of New England asters made by Mary Lou Smith of Wilbraham, Massachusetts. Her block was elegantly simple, using only five pieces, easily sewn, and it made spectacular asters.

Many different flowers can be made from this block, depending on your color and fabric choices: daisies, gazanias, fall asters, brown-eyed-Susans, etc.

The quilt can be homey or dramatically contemporary, depending on the fabrics selected for both the flower petals and for the background. Choices could be made to emphasize the set-in squares and their surrounding pinwheels as the primary design, with the flowers forming a more subdued pattern. It would be an interesting challenge for yourself or a group to make a number of small quilts from a block such as Painted Daisies, each having a very different impact from a varied set of fabric choices.

Piecing P4 with rectangular blocks is simple by hand but is a little more complicated on the machine. After the individual blocks are sewn, careful piecing is necessary to inset the squares.

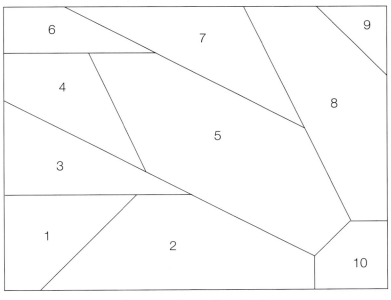

LAYOUT FOR PAINTED DAISY BLOCK

ASSEMBLY

Sew   1 to 2 to 3
        4 to 5 to 6 to 7
        8 to 9
        (1,2,3) to (4,5,6,7) to (8,9) to 10

QUILTING

Painted Daisies was hand quilted by Carol Marrochello, ¼" from the edge of the daisies and from the turquoise squares. The borders were quilted with a free-hand pattern of concentric arcs. Cotton batting.

LAYOUT FOR PAINTED DAISY QUILT

CHAPTER 4
PM ~ MIRROR SYMMETRY

Lily

■ ■ ■

With this chapter, we will begin to use reversed (mirrored) blocks along with our original ones.

To set out this symmetry, begin with a row of four blocks, arranged plain, mirror, plain, mirror, all with Side A at the top. Repeat this row three more times to make a square of sixteen.

A second pattern can be developed by beginning the layout with a row of four blocks, plain, mirror, plain, mirror, all with Side B at the top. Repeat this row three more times to make a square of sixteen.

The block I have drawn makes stylized lily blossoms when used in this symmetry. I used two off-white fabrics for the petals and a pale yellow plaid for the base of the petals; I made some strip-pieced fabric of green and the dark background, which I cut into rectangles for the borders.

The wallhanging I have sewn is composed of thirty

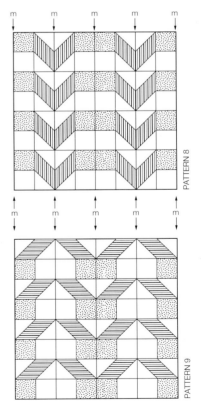

PATTERN 8

PATTERN 9

SYMMETRY NOTATION FOR PM

27

blocks cut from a single set of fabrics. Consider making a wallhanging from a shaded progression of flowers, such as white to pinks to burgundy. Or try one with lilies made from boldly streaked, colorful fabrics. This quilt would look very different if large-scale flowery chintzes were used for the background fabrics, giving an impression of a clump of lilies in a blooming perennial border.

TO MAKE THE QUILT ILLUSTRATED

Finished size: 48½" x 41" (123 x 104 cm)
30 Lily Blocks, 15 plain and 15 reversed: 7 x 5¼"

Color	TEMPLATE								
	1	2	2R	3	3R	4	4R	5	5R
White 1	-	15	15	-	-	-	-	15	15
White 2	-	-	-	-	-	-	-	-	-
Plaid	-	-	-	-	-	-	-	-	-
Background	30	-	-	15	15	15	15	-	-

Color	TEMPLATE								
	6	6R	7	8	9	10	10R	11	11R
White 1	-	-	-	-	-	-	-	-	-
White 2	-	-	-	30	-	-	-	-	-
Plaid	-	-	-	-	-	-	-	15	15
Background	15	15	30	-	30	15	15	-	-

Color	TEMPLATE	Yardage	Meters
	12		
White 1	-	½	0.5
White 2	30	⅝	0.625
Plaid	-	⅛	0.125
Background	-	1⅛	1.125

Borders

For the border, I strip-pieced a fabric from 1½"-wide strips of green and 1¼"-wide strips of background. From this fabric, I cut rectangles for the inner top and bottom borders:
Inner side borders: Cut 2 (3½" x 45½")
Bottom border: Cut 6 (7½" x 5¾")
Inner top border: Cut 6 (3½" x 3½")
Notice that the stripes are angled in opposite directions in the rectangles. Make sure to cut your rectangles accordingly. Use extreme caution in handling the rectangles, as the edges will all be on the bias.
From background fabric, I cut 2 (2" x 48") strips for side borders, and 6 (3½" x 2¾") rectangles for the inner top border, and 1 (3" x 38") strip for the top border.

Color	Yardage	Meters
Green	1	1
Background	1¼	1.25
Backing fabric	1½	1.5

QUILTING

Hand quilting was used in the center of the quilt, in the ditch around the lilies, and diagonally across the background. When sewing the blocks, press the seam allowances under the lily petals. This will make the lily pop up and the background recede when you quilt around the lily. Pale yellow hand quilting on petals 2 and 5 added more detail. The borders are machine quilted with a programmed stitch along the centers of the stripes, black thread used on the green stripes, and a slightly smaller version of the same programmed stitch with purple thread used on the dark stripes. Cotton batting.

ASSEMBLY

Sew   1 to 2 to 3
       4 to 5 to 6
       (1,2,3) to (4,5,6) to 12
       7 to 8 to 9
       10 to 11 to (7,8,9)
Join the sub-units.

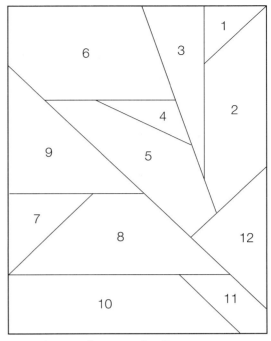

LAYOUT FOR LILY BLOCK

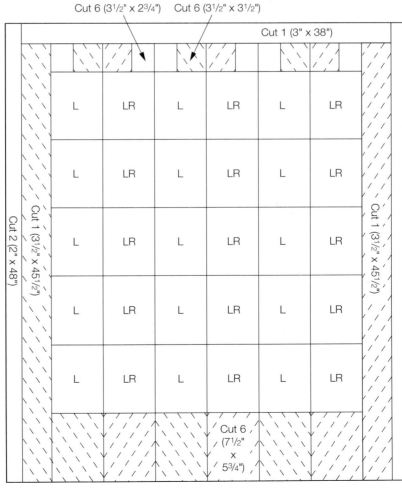

LAYOUT FOR LILY QUILT

29

Poppies

P2MM has two mirror lines at right angles to each other. In its symmetry, P2MM begins to resemble many traditional quilt patterns.

To lay out this symmetry with your paper blocks, make a group of four blocks as shown.

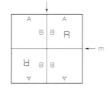

Basic group of Four With Double Mirror Lines

You will see the mirror lines vertically and horizontally through the center. Now repeat this group three more times to make a sixteen-block design.

The block I designed makes poppies when used in P2MM symmetry and has a little tuft of leaves of graduated sizes. The piecing is simple straight lines.

It is often effective to adapt a block design to border

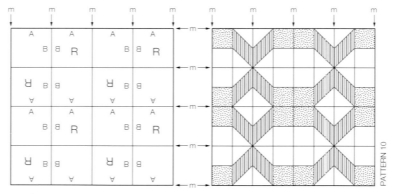

Symmetry Notation for P2MM

TO MAKE THE QUILT ILLUSTRATED

Finished size: 67½" x 42½" (171 x 108 cm)
32 Poppies Blocks, 16 plain and 16 reversed: 7" x 8"

Color	TEMPLATE								
	1	2	3	3R	4	4R	5	5R	6
Red 1	-	-	-	-	-	-	-	-	8
Red 2	-	-	-	-	-	-	-	-	-
Orange 1	-	-	-	-	-	-	-	-	8
Orange 2	-	-	-	-	-	-	-	-	-
Green 1	-	-	16	16	-	-	-	-	-
Green 2	-	-	-	-	16	16	-	-	-
Green 3	-	-	-	-	-	-	16	16	-
Blue purple	64	-	-	-	-	-	-	-	-
Center	-	-	-	-	-	-	-	-	-
Background	128	96	-	-	-	-	-	-	-

a quilt. For this Poppies quilt, I have used a shortened version of the original block for all the borders. Keeping the small green triangles in the borders consistent with the center blocks carries the rhythms of the central section out to the edge of the quilt. A color change in the petal fabrics in the borders, from the red-orange central blocks to mauves and purples, frames the piece without rigidly confining it.

| | TEMPLATE | | | | | |
Color	6R	7	7R	8	Yardage	Meters
Red 1	8	-	-	-	¼	0.25
Red 2	-	8	8	-	¼	0.25
Orange 1	8	-	-	-	¼	0.25
Orange 2	-	8	8	-	¼	0.25
Green 1	-	-	-	-	¼	0.25
Green 2	-	-	-	-	¼	0.25
Green 3	-	-	-	-	⅜	0.375
Blue purple	-	-	-	-	⅛	0.125
Center	-	-	-	32	¼	0.25
Background	-	-	-	-	⅝	0.675

Borders

The border of the poppies was made from two shortened versions of the poppies block.
For the side borders (PA), cut the block ¼ beyond Point A, as shown on page 32.

| | TEMPLATE | | | | | | | |
Color	3	3R	4	4R	5	5R	Yardage	Meters
Green 1	8	8	-	-	-	-	⅛	0.125
Green 2	-	-	8	8	-	-	¼	0.25
Green 3	-	-	-	-	8	8	¼	0.25
Color	1	2	6(A)	6R(A)				
Background	64	32	8	8			¼	0.25

For the top and bottom borders (PB), cut the block at Point B, as shown on page 32.

| | TEMPLATE | | | | | | | |
Color	1	2	6	6R	7(B)	7R(B)	8	Yardage	Meters
Brown	-	-	4	4	4	4	-	¼	0.25
Blue-purple	-	-	-	-	-	-	8	⅛	0.125
Background	24	8	-	-	-	-	-	⅜	0.375

Cut strips for the top and bottom 2 (3" x 42½") from the background fabric.

For the corner blocks (PAB), cut the block at Points A and B, as shown on page 32.

| | TEMPLATE | | | | |
Color	1	2	6(A)	6R(A)	
Blue-purple	-	-	2	2	(Yardage included in quantities above.)
Background	4	4	-	-	
Backing fabric				2	2

QUILTING

Using a variety of programmed machine stitches and threads of blue, green, and purple, the surface was quilted in concentric squares centered around the orange poppies. Cotton batting.

ASSEMBLY

Sew   1a to 3 to 1b to 5 to 1c
2a to 6
2b to 4 to 1d to (2a,6)
2c to 7 to (1a,3,1b,5,1c)
(1a,3,1b,5,1c,2c,7) to (2b,4,1d,2a,6)
1e to 8 to 1f
Join the sub-units.

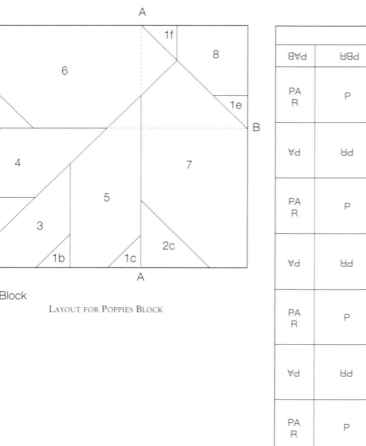

P
Poppy Block

LAYOUT FOR POPPIES BLOCK

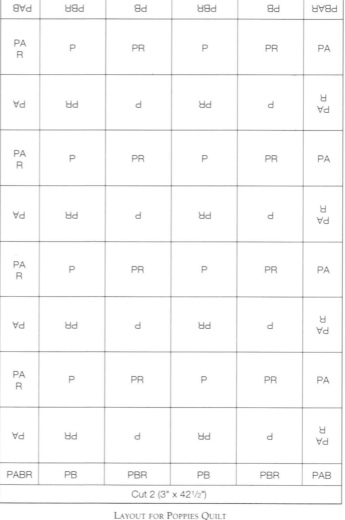

PAB	PBR	PB	PBR	PB	PBAR
PA R	P	PR	P	PR	PA
PA	PR	P	PR	P	PA R
PA R	P	PR	P	PR	PA
PA	PR	P	PR	P	PA R
PA R	P	PR	P	PR	PA
PA	PR	P	PR	P	PA R
PA R	P	PR	P	PR	PA
PA	PR	P	PR	P	PA R
PABR	PB	PBR	PB	PBR	PAB

Cut 2 (3" x 42½")

LAYOUT FOR POPPIES QUILT

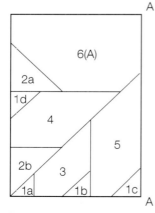

PA
Side Border

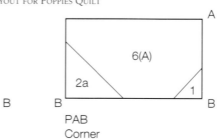

PB
Top and Bottom Borders

PAB
Corner

Masks

■ ■ ■

The mirrored pairs are staggered in this symmetry from one row to the next. The C in the label stands for "centered lattice" and shows up in this symmetry and the next one.

To lay out CM with your paper blocks, begin with a mirrored pair (plain block and mirror block, both with Side A at the top). Make another mirrored pair and place it next to the first to make a horizontal row. Now, make a third mirrored pair and center it in the next row under these four blocks. The third row repeats the first row, and the fourth repeats the second. A second pattern will develop if you begin with mirrored pairs with Side B at the top.

The block represents half of a mask. The mirrored pairs in CM symmetry will make complete masks.

Varying the fabric choices will make tremendous differences in the appearance of the faces. I have chosen batiked and primitive-looking fabrics.

Carnival colors might make a Mardi Gras quilt. Pale pastels and watercolor prints could be very romantic. Primary colors and white might fit a crayon-box color scheme. You could make a very contemporary wallhanging from blacks and whites, perhaps with solid red accents.

I have also chosen to make all of the plain blocks slightly lighter than the mirror or reversed blocks, giving the quilt a source of light and increasing the three-dimensional feeling. Since each template (except 12) is used for only one fabric, I have dispensed with the table format.

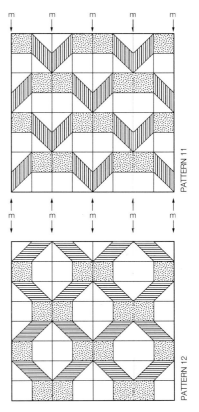

PATTERN 11

PATTERN 12

SYMMETRY NOTATION FOR CM

33

TO MAKE THE QUILT ILLUSTRATED

Finished size: 58½" x 70½" (148 x 179 cm)
48 Mask Blocks, 24 plain and 24 reversed: 12" x 5"

Color	TEMPLATE	Cut of each	Yardage	Meters
Eye (black)	1	48	¼	0.25
Face 1 light	2,3,4,6	24	¼	0.25
Face 1 dark	2R,3R,4R,6R	24	¼	0.25
Nose light	5	24	¼	0.25
Nose dark	5R	24	¼	0.25
Lips light	8	24	⅛	0.125
Lips dark	8R	24	⅛	0.125
Face 2 light	9, 10	24	¼	0.25
Face 2 dark	9R, 10R	24	¼	0.25
Face 3 light	11, 14	24	¾	0.75
Face 3 dark	11R, 14R	24	¾	0.75
Band light	7	24	¼	0.25
Band dark	7R	24	¼	0.25
Hair light	13, 15	24	¾	0.75
Hair dark	13R, 15R	24	¾	0.75
Background, light	12	48	⅜	0.375
Background, dark	12	48	⅜	0.375

Borders

Cut 2 (5½" x 48½") for side borders		1¾	1.75
Cut 2 (5½" x 60½") for top and bottom borders			
Cut 4 (5½" x 5½") corner blocks		¼	0.25
Backing fabric		3½	3.5

QUILTING

The masks are quilted free-motion by machine with a variegated red-yellow-blue rayon thread in a swirling pattern that almost resembles tattoos. It varies from face to face. In the border and on the background pieces, a continuous line of free-motion stitching makes a Greek key motif with occasional gables. Cotton batting.

ASSEMBLY

Sew   1 to 2 to 3 to 4 to 5 to 6
        8 to 9 to 10 to 11 to 12a
        (1,2,3,4,5,6) to (8,9,10,11,12a) to 7 to 13
        12b to 15 to 14
Join the sub-units.

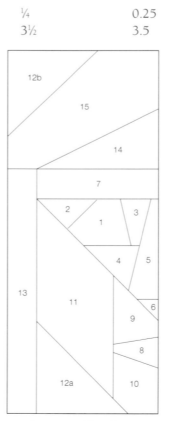

LAYOUT FOR MASK BLOCK

M	MR	M	MR	M	MR	M	MR	M	MR	M	MR
MR	M	MR	M	MR	M	MR	M	MR	M	MR	M
M	MR	M	MR	M	MR	M	MR	M	MR	M	MR
MR	M	MR	M	MR	M	MR	M	MR	M	MR	M

Cut 2 (5$\frac{1}{2}$" x 48$\frac{1}{2}$")

Cut 2 (5$\frac{1}{2}$" x 60$\frac{1}{2}$")

Cut 4 (5$\frac{1}{2}$" x 5$\frac{1}{2}$")

LAYOUT FOR MASK QUILT

LightningStrike

■ ■ ■

his is an unusual symmetry, similar to P2MM in that it contains the same mirrored groups of four blocks.

It also contains shifted rows, like CM.

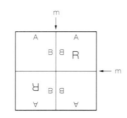

BASIC GROUP OF FOUR WITH DOUBLE MIRROR LINES

To lay C2MM out with your paper blocks, start with a group of four like the one shown above. Make another group of four and put the two groups together in a column. Now make a third group of four and

place it against the middle of the first column. A second pattern can also be developed by beginning the process with Side B at the top as shown.

It is characteristic of many C2MM patterns to have a large zigzag design between the vertical columns. I have chosen to emphasize that by making a lightning quilt. The block I have designed is very simple to piece using strip-piecing techniques, or it can be pieced in the traditional way with seven templates. Strip piecing is quicker, but it uses more fabric.

The patterned fabrics used in this quilt have a very significant impact on carrying out the lightning theme. The large-scale drapery print used in the outer border, containing as it does hints of yellows, pinks, and browns, along with gray and blue, works to carry the colors of the central pieced blocks into the border.

An inner border of bands of colors, butted rather

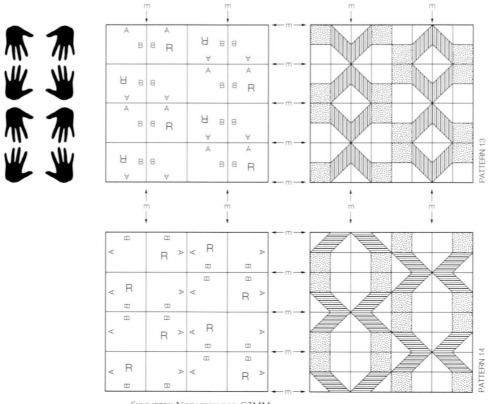

SYMMETRY NOTATION FOR C2MM

PATTERN 13

PATTERN 14

TO MAKE THE QUILT ILLUSTRATED

Finished size: 78½" x 44" (199 x 112 cm)

36 Lightning Strike Blocks, 18 plain and 18 reversed: 6" x 7½"

To strip piece this quilt, cut six strips across the width of the fabric, of the colors and dimensions below.

Color	Strip Width	Yardage	Meters
Yellow	1¾"	¼	0.25
Black 1	2½"	½	0.5
Sew these together and cut 36 of Template 1.			
Cloudy blue	3¾"	¾	0.75
Black 2	1¼"	¼	0.25
Beige	2"	⅜	0.375
Blue	2⅝"	½	0.5
Gray white	2¾"	½	0.5
Sew these together in the order indicated and cut 18 of Template 2 and 18 of Template 2R.			

Borders			
Blue cloud		½	0.5
Cut 2 (3" x 33") for first top and bottom borders			
Cut 2 (1¾" x 54½") for first side borders			
Yellow		⅛	0.125
Cut 2 (2" x 33") for second top and bottom borders			
Black		⅛	0.125
Cut 1 (1" x 33") for third bottom border			
Outer clouds		1	1
Cut 2 (8" x 44") for outer top and bottom borders			
Cut 2 (6" x 63") for outer side borders			
Backing fabric		3¼	3.25

than mitered at the corners, and varying top to bottom, was suggested to me by studying the bordering on oriental scroll paintings.

QUILTING

A free-motion machine stitched pattern of arcs and clouds, done by eye without previous marking, was stitched in a continuous line across the whole surface with black thread. It reinforces for me the turmoil of a thunderstorm. Cotton batting.

ASSEMBLY

Sew   1 to 2

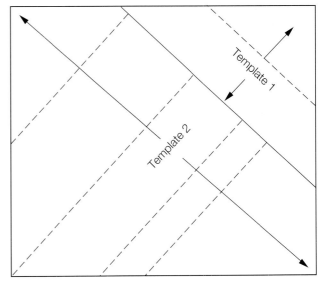

LAYOUT FOR LIGHTNING STRIKE BLOCK

37

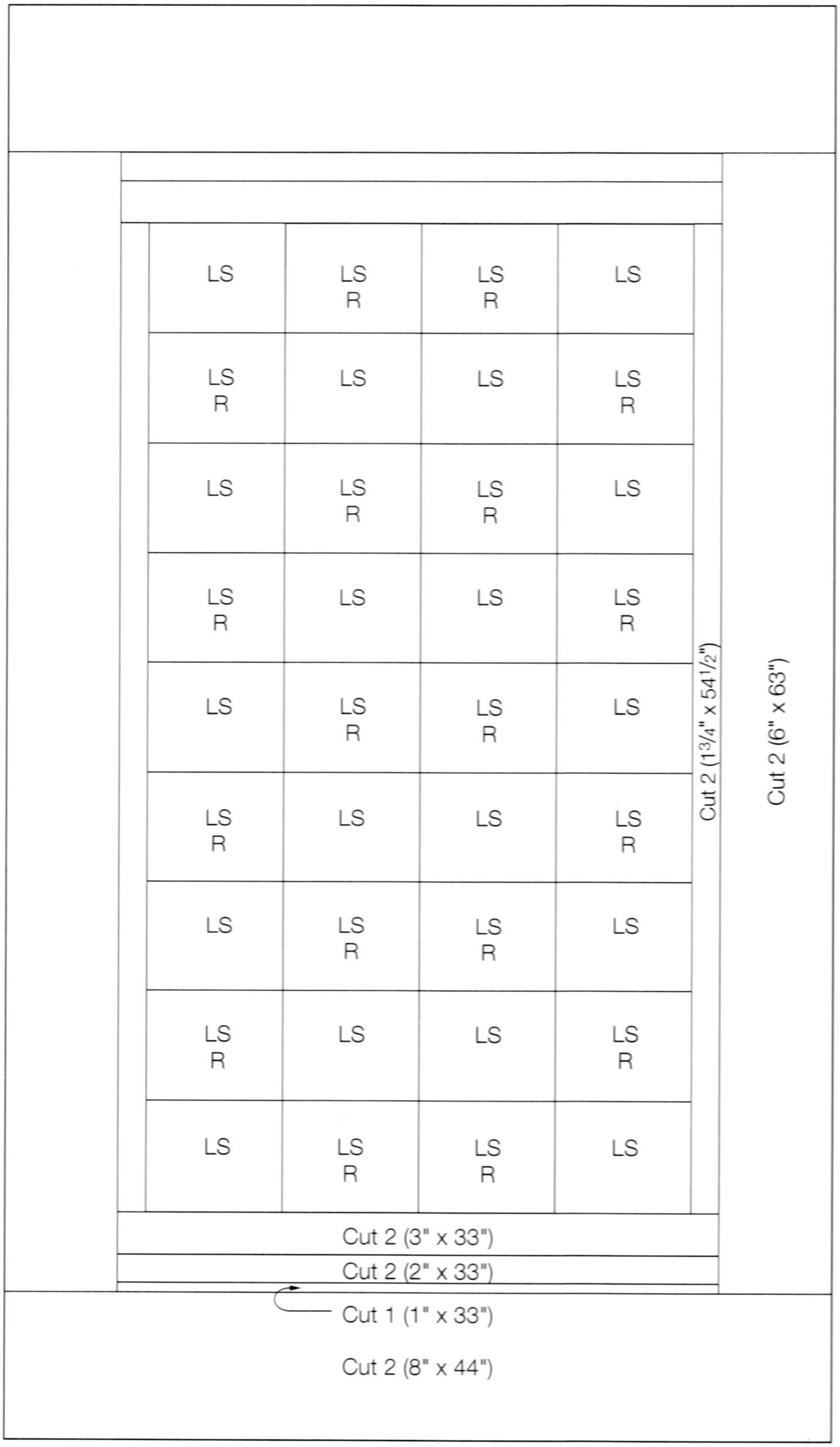

LS	LS R	LS R	LS
LS R	LS	LS	LS R
LS	LS R	LS R	LS
LS R	LS	LS	LS R
LS	LS R	LS R	LS
LS R	LS	LS	LS R
LS	LS R	LS R	LS
LS R	LS	LS	LS R
LS	LS R	LS R	LS

Cut 2 (1³⁄₄" x 54¹⁄₂")

Cut 2 (6" x 63")

Cut 2 (3" x 33")

Cut 2 (2" x 33")

Cut 1 (1" x 33")

Cut 2 (8" x 44")

LAYOUT FOR LIGHTNING STRIKE QUILT

KatsuraLeaves

■ ■ ■

In this chapter we meet glide symmetry. Although both plain and mirror blocks are used, there are no mirror lines: you can't arrive at this symmetry by placing a mirror along any of the edges of the unit block. I have often used this symmetry very successfully in my art quilts, but have never found it in an antique quilt.

To lay out PG with your paper blocks, begin with a row of four plain blocks, all with Side A at the top. Underneath this row, make a row of four mirror blocks, with Side A at the top. Repeat these two rows.

A second pattern will develop if you place the rows with Side B at the top.

Katsura trees have small heart-shaped leaves which turn red in the Fall. I had a lot of fun making the leaves from a variety of red fabrics, throwing in some pinks, orange, and yellow for spice. Striped fabrics were cut so that the stripes echoed the veins in the leaves.

There is an interrupted lattice effect produced by the teal background pieces. I have often used the back-and-forth motion of PG symmetry very successfully in quilts inspired by leaves and vines.

The block is simple to piece, although it uses eight templates.

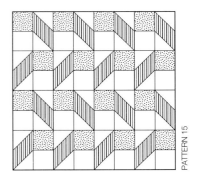

PATTERN 15

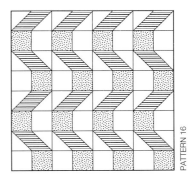

PATTERN 16

SYMMETRY NOTATION FOR **PG**

39

TO MAKE THE QUILT ILLUSTRATED

Finished size: 83½" x 61½" (213 x 156 cm)
48 Katsura Leaf Blocks: 9" x 9"

TEMPLATES

Color	7	7R	8	8R	Yardage	Meters
Leaf	24	24	24	24	2	2
	5	5R	6	6R		
Teal	24	24	48	48	¾	0.75
	1	2	3	4		
Background	48	96	48	96	¾	0.75

Borders		
Teal	1⅝	1.675
Cut 2 (2" x 54½") for first top and bottom borders		
Gray	1⅝	1.675
Cut 2 (4½" x 54½") for outer top and bottom borders	¾	0.75
Cut 2 (4" x 83½") for outer side borders		
Backing fabric	3¾	3.75

QUILTING

An angular pattern of veins, machine stitched with an even-feed foot and gray thread, serves as the quilting pattern. To mark the quilting lines, I cut a stencil from template plastic based on the quilting diagram and marked it on each pieced leaf with a chalk pencil. Cotton batting. Enlarge quilting design on page 120 to 111%.

ASSEMBLY

Sew   1 to 7 to 4a to 4b
          2b to 6
          2a to 8 to 5
          3 to 6R
          (2b,6) to (2a,8,5) to (3,6R)
Join the sub-units.

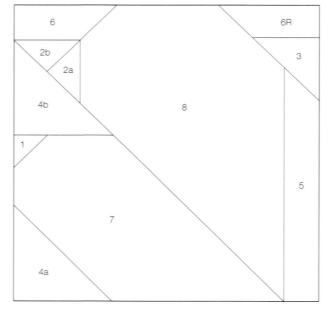

LAYOUT FOR KATSURA LEAF BLOCK

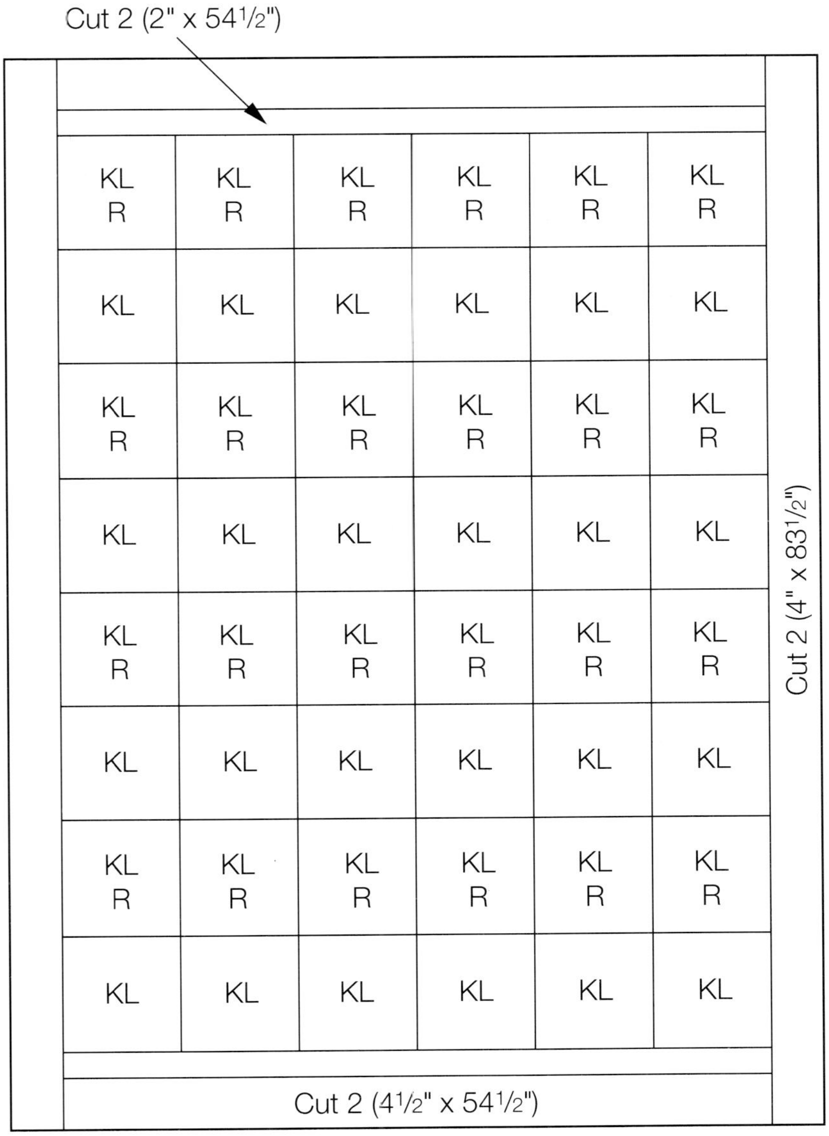

Cut 2 (2" x 54½")

KL R	KL R	KL R	KL R	KL R	KL R
KL	KL	KL	KL	KL	KL
KL R	KL R	KL R	KL R	KL R	KL R
KL	KL	KL	KL	KL	KL
KL R	KL R	KL R	KL R	KL R	KL R
KL	KL	KL	KL	KL	KL
KL R	KL R	KL R	KL R	KL R	KL R
KL	KL	KL	KL	KL	KL

Cut 2 (4" x 83½")

Cut 2 (4½" x 54½")

LAYOUT FOR KATSURA LEAF QUILT

CHAPTER 9
P2GG ~ Two Glides

DecoMoon

∎ ∎ ∎

The effect of this symmetry is very much like confetti. To lay out the pattern with your paper blocks, start with a row of four plain blocks, alternating Side A at the top, then Side A at the bottom. The second row is all mirror blocks, alternating Side A at the top, then Side A at the bottom. If you look at the columns of the resulting pattern, you will see that the first and third column match PG; in the second and fourth column, each block has been turned upside-down.

The Deco Moon quilt is a good place to practice your curved seam piecing. The block sews together easily, especially if you mark dots where indicated on each piece of fabric cut from Templates 1, 2, 3, and 4,

and pin the dots together before sewing. A small hole punched in a plastic template, as indicated in the templates, will allow you to locate the dots accurately.

I varied the color of half of the blocks to give the surface more interest, while keeping the blue and white (Templates 1 and 2) consistent.

I enjoy using borders with corner blocks, both as a reference back to traditional quilts and for the chance to insert some small squares of color into the border to complement and contrast with the pieced blocks.

The scale of the borders is important to unify the quilt and give a feeling of completion and balance. The border and quilting I've chosen for Deco Moon are just about perfect in setting off these pieced blocks.

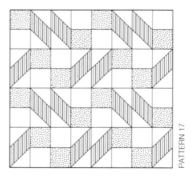

PATTERN 17

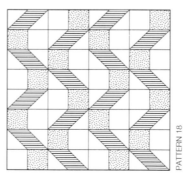

PATTERN 18

SYMMETRY NOTATION FOR **P2GG**

42

TO MAKE THE QUILT ILLUSTRATED

Finished size: 55" x 49" (140 x 125 cm)
24 Deco Moon Blocks, 12 plain and 12 reversed: 5" x 9"

Color	1	1R	2	2R	3	3R	Yardage	Meters
White	12	12	-	-	-	-	¼	0.25
Blue	-	-	12	12	-	-	¼	0.25
Gray/brown	-	-	-	-	12	12	⅝	0.625
	4	4R	5	5R			Yardage	Meters
Red	12	12	-	-			¼	0.25
Green	-	-	12	12			¼	0.25

Borders

Black	Cut 2 (4¼" x 30½") for first top and bottom borders	½	0.5
	Cut 2 (4¼" x 36½") for first side borders		
Red	Cut 2 (2" x 38") for second top and bottom borders	¼	0.25
	Cut 2 (2" x 44") for second side borders		
Green	Cut 2 (4½" x 47") for outer side borders	⅝	0.625
	Cut 2 (4½" x 49") for outer top and bottom borders		

Corner Blocks

Turquoise	Cut 4 (4¼" x 4¼")	⅛	0.125
Blue	Cut 4 (2" x 2")	⅛	0.125
Backing fabric		3¼	3.25

QUILTING

Deco Moon reminded me of some Amish quilts I have seen, which are often elaborately hand quilted with feathers and wreaths. I marked freehand the sinuous lines that form the spines of the feathers in the border with a chalk pencil, then free-motion quilted the feather pattern with machine stitching in black. To quilt the blocks, I selected a contrasting angular free-motion quilting pattern that forms an angled grid where it crosses the moons. Cotton batting.

ASSEMBLY

Sew   1 to 2 to 3 to 4 to 5

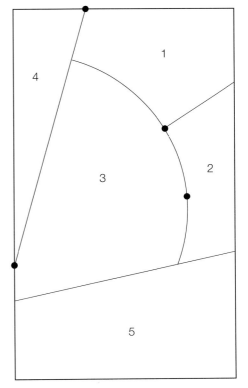

LAYOUT FOR DECO MOON BLOCK

43

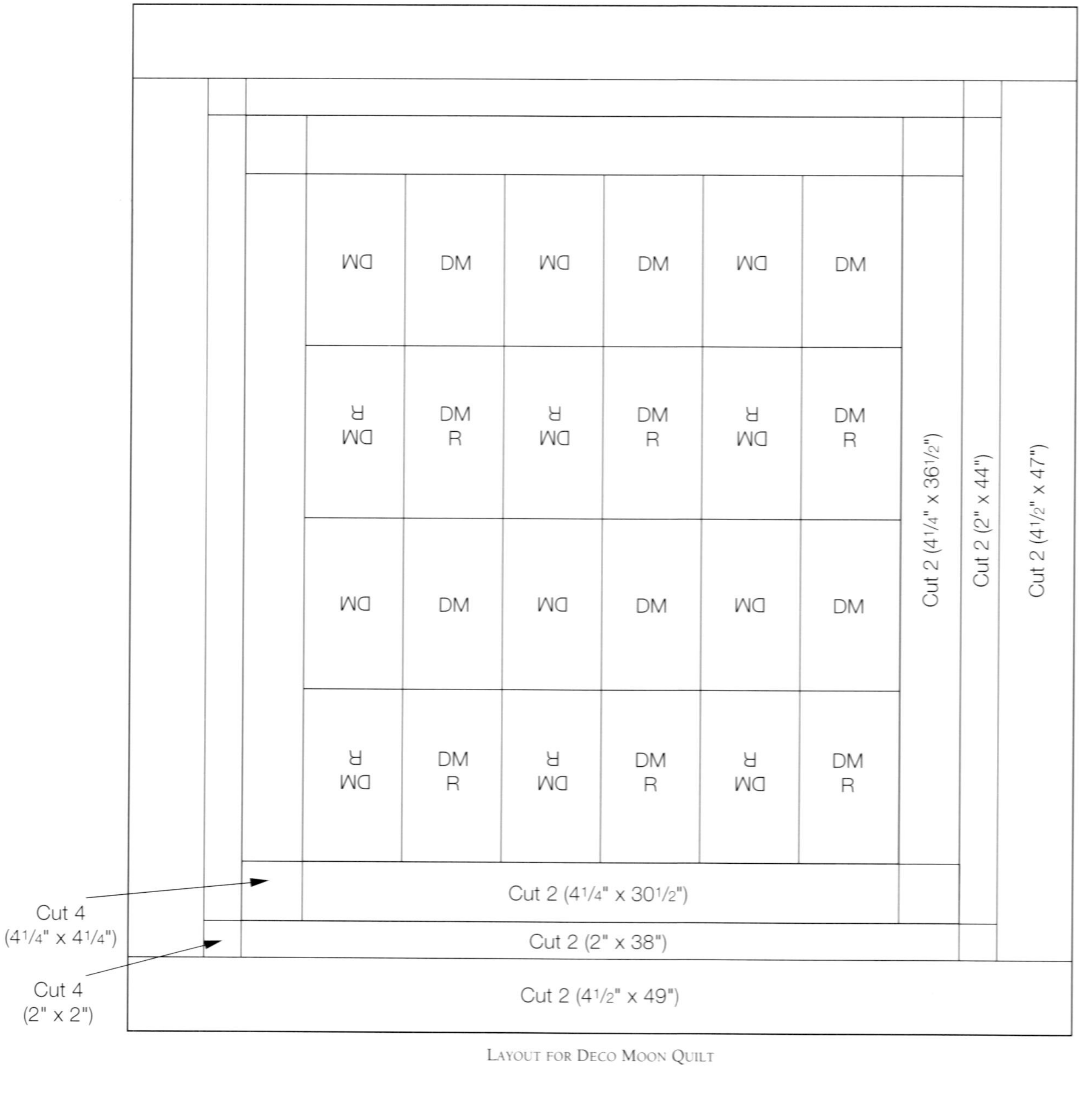

DM	DM	DM	DM	DM	DM
DM R	DM R	DM R	DM R	DM R	DM R
DM	DM	DM	DM	DM	DM
DM R	DM R	DM R	DM R	DM R	DM R

Cut 2 (4¼" x 36½")

Cut 2 (2" x 44")

Cut 2 (4½" x 47")

Cut 2 (4¼" x 30½")

Cut 2 (2" x 38")

Cut 2 (4½" x 49")

Cut 4
(4¼" x 4¼")

Cut 4
(2" x 2")

LAYOUT FOR DECO MOON QUILT

CHAPTER 10
P2MG ~ GLIDES AND MIRRORS

SchoolofFish

■ ■ ■

Every time I have taught symmetry to a roomful of students, at least one of their paper blocks makes a design that looks like fish swimming in opposite directions when we get to P2MG symmetry. For this chapter, I deliberately set out to make a block that would produce fish.

With your paper blocks, follow the diagrams sketched below. Again, there are two patterns to find.

In many ways, this is the most elaborate of the quilts in the book. The fish are enlivened with inserted quilted three-dimensional "free fins" and double button eyes.

Drawing blocks for piecing particular images always presents a series of compromises. Here I set out to use P2MG symmetry to make schools of fish swimming in opposite directions. Each fish would be com-

posed of parts of four blocks. But the other parts of these same four blocks simultaneously make parts of five other fish swimming in the opposite direction.

In drawing this design I simultaneously drew both opposing schools of fish. At the same time, I tried to make the piecing simple and the templates of a manageable size. But I still wanted to make the fish look like fish. Because I couldn't stand for the fish to have pointy noses, I decided to add the little triangles of Template 1, which are smaller than most quilters are used to handling. However, once you have sewn the pieces from Template 1 to those from Template 2, the tiny piecing is finished and you will be working with a simple piecing pattern. As I describe, you will then sew 3 to 4 to 5 to 6 to 7 to 8 and finally sew the 1, 2 triangle to these to complete the block.

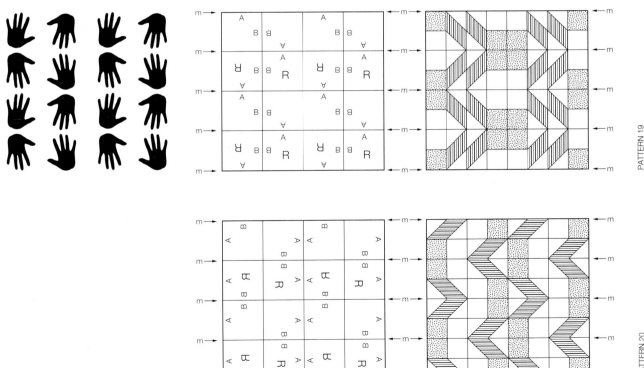

PATTERN 19

PATTERN 20

SYMMETRY NOTATION FOR P2MG

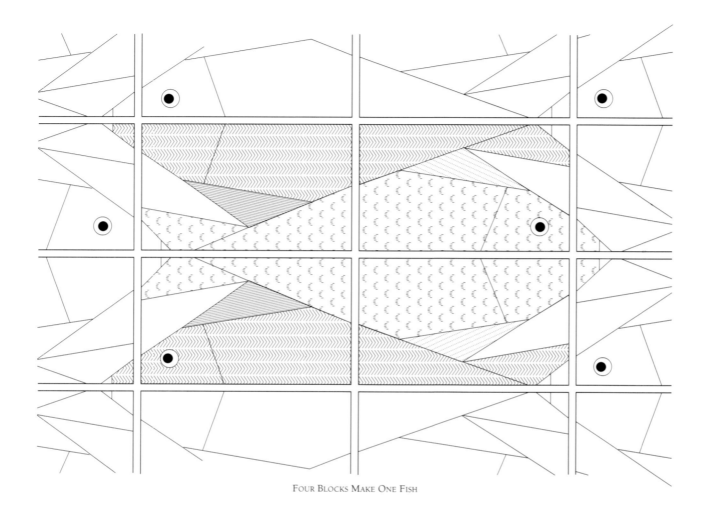

FOUR BLOCKS MAKE ONE FISH

TO MAKE THE QUILT ILLUSTRATED
Finished size: 77½" x 101" (197 x 256 cm)
80 School of Fish Blocks, 40 plain and 40 reversed: 6" x 10"

					TEMPLATE					
Color	1	2	2R	3	3R	4	4R	5	5R	6
Fish head	-	40	40	-	-	40	40	-	-	-
Fish body	-	-	-	40	40	-	-	-	-	-
Tail	-	-	-	-	-	-	-	-	-	-
Blue fin	-	-	-	-	-	-	-	40	40	-
Blue sea	80	-	-	-	-	-	-	-	-	40
Free fins	-	-	-	-	-	-	-	-	-	-

Color	6R	7	7R	8	8R	Yardage	Meters
			TEMPLATE				
Fish head	-	-	-	-	-	2	2
Fish body	-	-	-	40	40	3	3
Tail	-	40	40	-	-	1	1
Blue fin	-	-	-	-	-	1⅛	1.125
Blue sea	40	-	-	-	-	⅞	0.675
Free fins	-	20	20	-	-	½	0.5

Free fins

Sew the pieces cut from the modified Template 7, right sides together, in pairs with a ¼" seam, leaving the end open. Clip the corners. Turn and press. Quilt by hand or machine.

When the blocks have been sewn together and you decide on the placement of the free fins, rip a small space in the seam between the head and the body and slip the unfinished edge of the free fin into the space. Resew the seam, catching the free fin in place.

Borders

The outer border on School of Fish used almost every scrap of a cotton pareu I found on St. Maarten after I had finished making the center of the quilt. The pareu, a hand-painted scene of tropical fish, was about two yards long and was cut and pieced together to set the ocean stage for my school.

The side inner borders have been pieced to complete the heads of the fish that are swimming out of the quilt.

Color	1	2	2R	9	9R	Yardage	Meters
			TEMPLATE				
Fish head	-	10	10	-	-	½	0.5
Blue sea	20	-	-	10	10	½	0.5
Blue print						1	1
Cut 2 (4" x 85½") for top and bottom inner borders							
Cut 2 (2" x 67½") for side middle border							
Pareu						2	2
Cut 1 (5" x 88½") for top outer border							
Cut 1 (6" x 88½") for bottom outer border							
Cut 2 (6¾" x 77½") for side outer borders							
Backing fabric						5¾	5.75

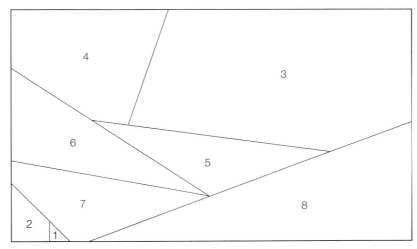

LAYOUT FOR SCHOOL OF FISH BLOCK

QUILTING

My School of Fish was quilted on the machine by free motion with black thread. I first quilted in the ditch around each fish, then went back and drew in scales, eyes, and mouths with the free-motion stitching. The borders were quilted by free motion outlining the fish, seaweed, and coral, and I carried the printed design onto the plain fabric where it was cut by the edge of the border. Since the quilt is very large, you may want to consider quilting it in sections (quilt-as-you-go), then sewing it together. Cotton batting.

ASSEMBLY

Sew   1 to 2
           3 to 4 to 5 to 6 to 7 to 8 to (1, 2)

EMBELLISHMENT

- 20 white pearl buttons, 1" diameter
- 20 black plastic buttons, ½" diameter

Sew a black button on top of a white button to make eyes for the quilted fish. Consider rummaging through an old button box for something appropriate. It's okay if the eyes don't all match: the variety will give character to the fish.

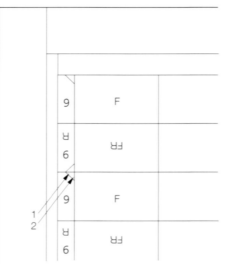

INNER BORDERS WITH FISH HEADS

LAYOUT FOR SCHOOL OF FISH QUILT

SpinningRings

The pattern for this symmetry is a checkerboard of plain and mirror pinwheels. There will be four different patterns for square blocks, depending on which corner is placed at the center of the pinwheel. With rectangular blocks, there are eight different patterns; they require the addition of rectangles or squares to fill out the surface.

Let's begin with square blocks. To start, make two pinwheels of plain blocks with Corner 1 in the center of the pinwheels. Make two pinwheels of mirror blocks with Corner 1 in the center. Arrange these four pinwheels in a checkerboard pattern as shown on page 50. You will notice a mirror line vertically and horizontally through the center of these patterns.

If you place Corner 2, Corner 3, or Corner 4 in the center of each pinwheel, you will find three other patterns.

With rectangular blocks, the situation is more complicated. Begin by making a pinwheel of four plain rectangular blocks with Corner 1 touching in the center of the pinwheel. Make another pinwheel the same. Now, make two pinwheels of mirror blocks with Corner 1 touching in the center of the pinwheels. Arrange the four pinwheels as in the first diagram on page 51.

You will find large open rectangles, between the pinwheels, moving back and forth in a basket-weave pattern. These can be filled with a solid piece of fabric or another type of design.

There are three other patterns of this type with Corner 2, Corner 3, or Corner 4 in the center of the pinwheels. Notice the mirror lines vertically and horizontally through the center of these patterns.

If you make pinwheels of rectangular blocks centered around a square, the symmetry fits together more easily. The dimensions of the center square will be the difference between the lengths of the sides of the rectangular block.

The pinwheel of four blocks will have a square as its outer edge, with a side length equal to the sum of the two sides of the rectangular block.

Again, there will be four patterns, depending on which corner of the rectangular block is at the center of the pinwheels. See the layouts on page 52.

Notice the mirror lines vertically and horizontally in the center of these patterns.

The traditional Double Wedding Ring quilt has been made thousands of times. It is awkward to piece, especially by machine. As a design, it is very placid and stable. Most marriages, I suspect, are much more dynamic and full of compromise, hence Spinning Rings.

The Spinning Rings quilt I have made began with a center group of sixteen blocks, surrounded by a row of twenty blocks of a second color scheme, and another row of twenty-eight blocks of a third color scheme. A simplified block, using three templates, was used as a border.

One of the beauties of the Spinning Rings block is that it can be easily expanded to any size and even be made rectangular. The choice of fabrics in the pinwheels (Templates 2, 3, and 4) can blend with the background, or blend with the rings, or be bright spots of color to form a prominent design of their own.

For a bed quilt, the outer edge can be scalloped by leaving off Template 10. For a scalloped border, make sure you cut a bias binding.

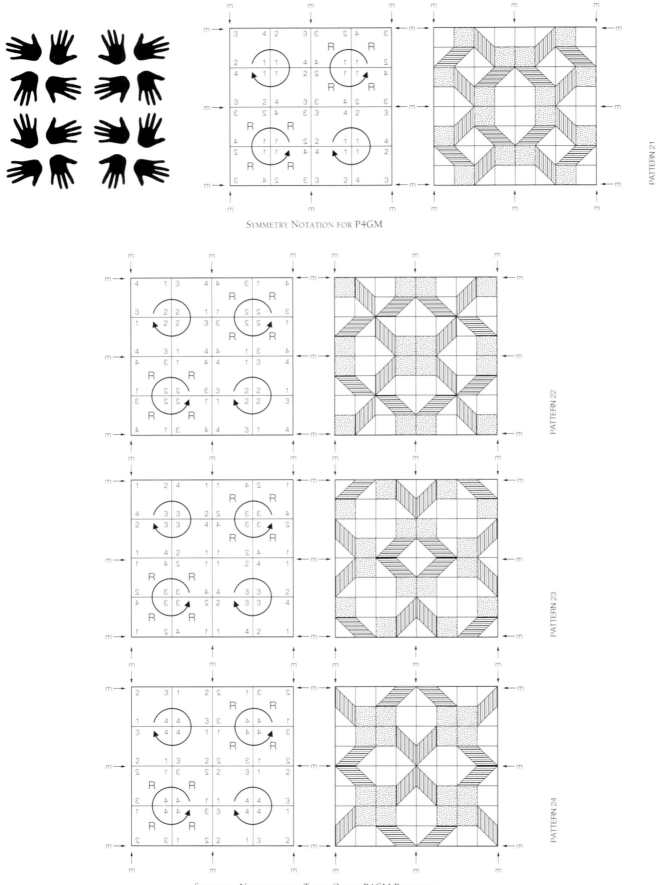

SYMMETRY NOTATION FOR P4GM

PATTERN 21

PATTERN 22

PATTERN 23

PATTERN 24

SYMMETRY NOTATION FOR THREE OTHER P4GM PATTERNS

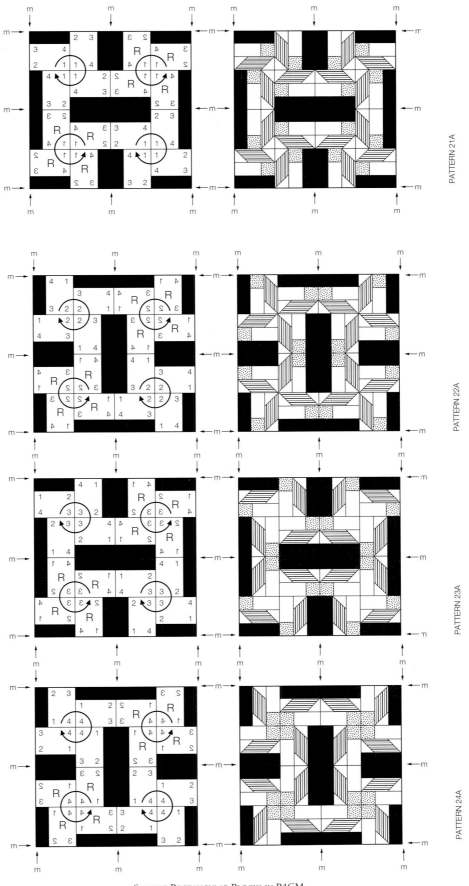

PATTERN 21A

PATTERN 22A

PATTERN 23A

PATTERN 24A

SETTING RECTANGULAR BLOCKS IN P4GM

51

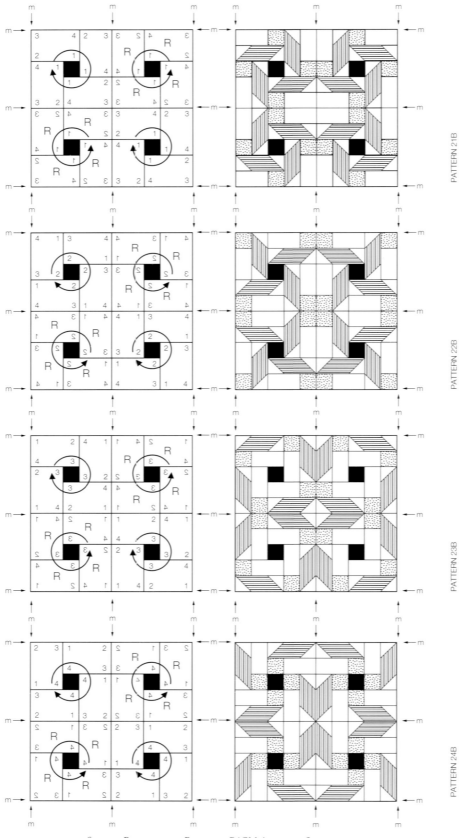

PATTERN 21B

PATTERN 22B

PATTERN 23B

PATTERN 24B

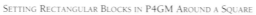

SETTING RECTANGULAR BLOCKS IN P4GM AROUND A SQUARE

52

TO MAKE THE QUILT ILLUSTRATED

Finished size: 72½" x 72½" (184 x 184 cm)
64 Spinning Rings Blocks: 6" x 6"

Color							Yardage	Meters
Rings	6	6R	8	8R			Yardage	Meters
Center	8	8	8	8			¼	0.25
Next row	10	10	10	10			⅜	0.375
Outer row	14	14	14	14			⅜	0.375
Pinwheels	2	2R	3	3R	4	4R	Yardage	Meters
Center	8	8	8	8	8	8	¼	0.25
Next row	10	10	10	10	10	10	¼	0.25
Outer row	14	14	14	14	14	14	⅜	0.375
Background	1	1R	5	5R	7	7R	Yardage	Meters
Center	8	8	8	8	8	8	¼	0.25
Next row	10	10	10	10	10	10	¼	0.25
Outer row	14	14	14	14	14	14	⅝	0.625

Header for first two rows spans: **Color** ... **TEMPLATE**

Borders	8	8R	9	9R	10	10R	Yardage	Meters
Blue	36	36	-	-	-	-	1½	1.5
Brown	-	-	36	36	36	36	2¼	2.25
Corner Blocks								
Cut 8 corner blocks (6½" x 6½")							½	0.5
Backing fabric							4¼	4.25

Header for Borders table: **Borders** ... **TEMPLATE**

QUILTING

Quilting on Spinning Rings was done by machine, with an even feed foot and light brown thread repeating the arcs of the rings. Cotton batting.

DOUBLE RINGS

The quilt can also be made with a pair of rings in the center, shown in the sketch on page 57. In this case, the quilt will be rectangular.

ASSEMBLY

Sew   1 to 2 to 3
          4 to 5 to 6 to 7
          (1, 2, 3) to 8 to (4, 5, 6, 7)
Sew   9 to 8 to 10

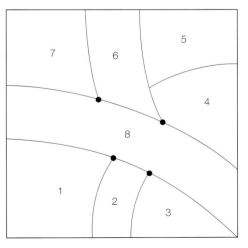

LAYOUT FOR SPINNING RINGS BLOCK (R)

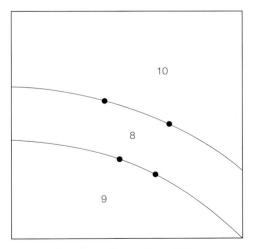

LAYOUT FOR BORDER BLOCK (RB)

Cut 8
(6½" x 6½")

	RB	RB	RB	RB	RB	RB	RB	RB	RB	
RB		RB R	RB	RB R	RB	RB R	RB	RB R	RB	RB R
RB R	RB	R	R	RR	RR	R	R	RR	RR	RB R	RB
RB	RB R	R	R	RR	RR	R	R	RR	RR	RB	RB R
RB R	RB	RR	RR	R	R	RR	RR	R	R	RB R	RB
RB	RB R	RR	RR	R	R	RR	RR	R	R	RB	RB R
RB R	RB	R	R	RR	RR	R	R	RR	RR	RB R	RB
RB	RB R	R	R	RR	RR	R	R	RR	RR	RB	RB R
RB R	RB	RR	RR	R	R	RR	RR	R	R	RB R	RB
RB	RB R	RR	RR	R	R	RR	RR	R	R	RB	RB R
RB R		RB	RB R	RB	RB R	RB	RB R	RB	RB R		RB
	RB	RB R	RB	RB R	RB	RB R	RB	RB R	RB	RB R

LAYOUT FOR SPINNING RINGS QUILT

FURTHER ADVENTURES WITH PART 1 BLOCKS

Each of the eleven blocks I have drawn for the Part 1 quilts can be used in all of the other symmetry patterns from Part 1. Some of the possibilities are illustrated below. In each case, using whatever block you choose, follow the symmetry notation diagrams. It may be helpful to label your selected block with Sides A and B and Corners 1, 2, 3, and 4, as I describe in the workshop directions. Spinning Rings block, for instance, will make three different designs in P4GM symmetry, if the other three corners of this square block are used in the center of the pinwheels.

SPINNING RINGS VARIATIONS, P4GM SYMMETRY

Many of the symmetries have two or more patterns, as illustrated in the symmetry notation diagrams. For instance, there are two patterns for P2MG symmetry: one pattern is drawn with Side A of each block at the top of the first row, the other with Side B at the top. Another School of Fish quilt could be made with the same School of Fish block, the same P2MG symmetry, but following the second of the diagrams instead. In this case, however, the "fish" disappear.

I've illustrated some of these other arrangements below. There are probably hundreds to choose from.

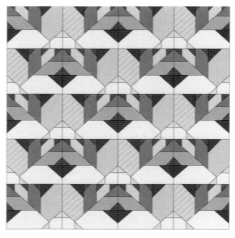

POPPIES BLOCK IN CM SYMMETRY

A SECOND PATTERN OF P2MG MADE WITH SCHOOL OF FISH BLOCK

YELLOW LILIES BLOCK IN P4GM SYMMETRY

MUSICAL NOTATION BLOCK ARRANGED AS P4 WITH
YELLOW FILLING SQUARES

SKETCH FOR A DOUBLE RINGS QUILT

SPINNING RINGS VARIATIONS, P4GM SYMMETRY

A Second Pattern of P2MG Made With School of Fish Blocks

POPPIES BLOCKS IN CM SYMMETRY

YELLOW LILIES BLOCK IN P4GM SYMMETRY

MUSICAL NOTATION BLOCK ARRANGED AS P4 WITH YELLOW FILLING SQUARES

SCRAMBLE DIAMOND BLOCK IN P2 SYMMETRY

RIGHT TRIANGULAR FROG BLOCK IN P4GM SYMMETRY

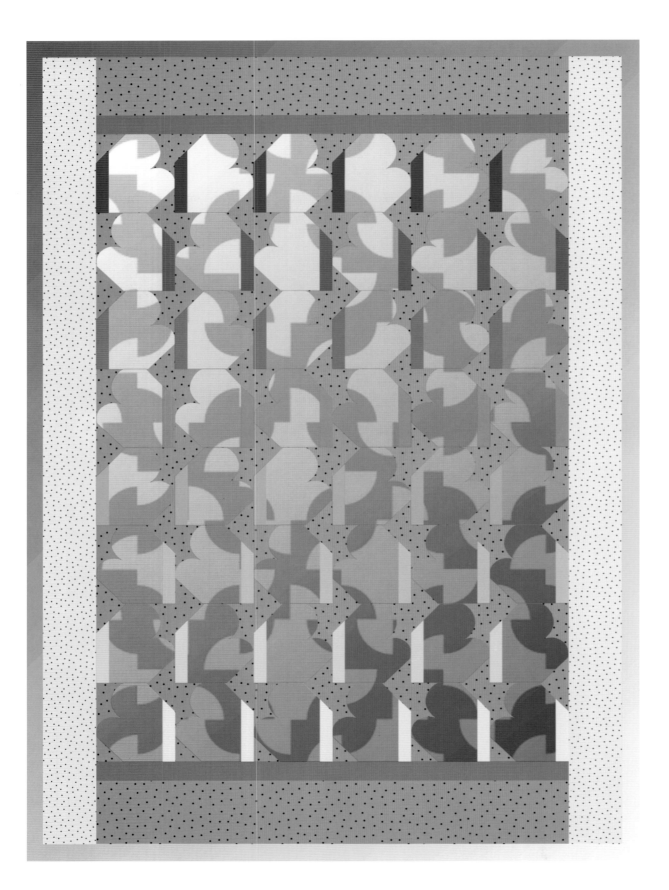

PartTwo

The six remaining symmetries fit together more easily as quilts if you use blocks other than squares or rectangles. For each of these six, I have chosen a simple shape which will fit together in that symmetry, and each of these is illustrated with a quilt. Using a process similar to the one you used in creating your square or rectangular paper block for Part 1, you can create original asymmetric designs for these symmetries as well. Simply start with the block shape indicated and, within it, make a simple asymmetric design.

Some of the symmetries from Part 1 can be laid out with blocks of these or other shapes, besides the square or rectangular blocks you've tried. See, for example, the two drawings in "Playing with Part 2 Blocks."

It is possible, I think, that some of these six remaining symmetries can be laid out with quilt block shapes other than the ones I have chosen for this book. Here's an opportunity for those who need a real challenge to investigate.

CHAPTER 12

P3 ~ 120° ROTATION

Scramble

■ ■ ■

The block for this quilt is a 60°-120° diamond, the same diamond that forms the traditional Baby Block quilt pattern. Three blocks fit together with the 120° corners in the center to form a hexagon. The hexagons then fit together to form the surface.

There are two different three-way pinwheels in this pattern, one where Corner 2's meet, and one where Corner 4's meet; there is a more complicated pinwheel composed of alternating Corner 1's and 3's.

The quilt illustrated is pieced from a block that contains one scrambling child. This is a complicated block to assemble, requiring 30 templates, and it has Y-seams at three places. It is recommended only for the experienced piecer.

The children can be given long hair or short hair simply by cutting Templates 6 and 7 from hair fabric or from background fabric.

Rather than covering the entire quilt with pieced blocks, I made only sixteen, filling out the surface with solid pieces of fabric, similar to the use of alternate plain blocks in many traditional quilts. These filling pieces are cut from Template 31, an equilateral triangle made from half of the Baby Block diamond, and Template 32, a scalene triangle made from half of Template 31, and which fills out the top and bottom edges. Template 33 is for the inner borders.

For this quilt, the figures are of darker values, with plaid shirts and indigo-dyed jeans; the background pieces are light. Other color schemes you might consider: a dark background with bright primary colors for the figures (Watch the value contrast between the hair and the background!); a colorful background emphasizing the three-way pinwheels where the corners of the blocks meet; or even, for fun, trying a variety of novelty fabrics — cars, people, animals, houses, chili peppers, whatever.

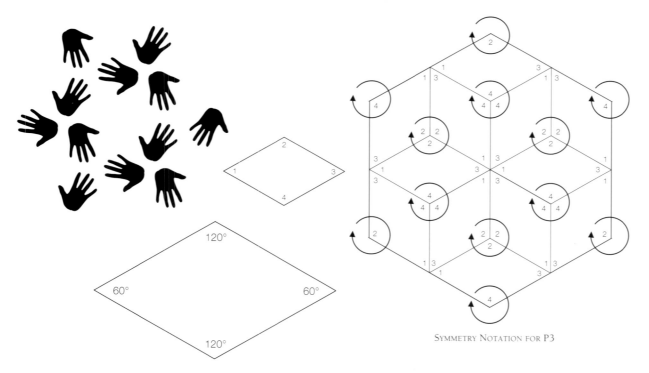

SYMMETRY NOTATION FOR P3

TO MAKE THE QUILT ILLUSTRATED
Finished size: 72¾" x 82½" (185 x 210 cm)
16 Scramble Blocks: 12" 60°-120° Diamond

TEMPLATE

Color			Yardage	Meters
Face	**1** Cut 16		⅛	0.125
Hands	**9 13** Cut 16		⅛	0.125
Feet	**20 28** Cut 16		⅛	0.125
Shirt	**10 14 16 19** Cut 16		⅜	0.375
Jeans	**23 24 26** Cut 16		½	0.5
Hair	**2** Cut 16		⅛	0.125
	6 7 (Cut 16 for long hair)			
Neck	**5** Cut 16		⅛	0.125
Background			5	5
	6 7 (Cut 16 for short hair)			
	3 4 8 11, 12 Cut 16			
	15 17 18 21 22 Cut 16			
	25 27 29 30 Cut 16			
	31 Cut 34			
	32 32R Cut 6			

Borders
An inner border of triangles (Template 33) was cut from many fabrics and sewn together randomly in a long strip. The strip was then cut into a top and bottom border 62¾" long and side borders 72½" long.

Multi	**Template 33** Cut 190	1	1
Blue print		¾	0.75
	Cut 2 (3" x 77½") for outer side borders		
	Cut 2 (3" x 72¾") for outer top and bottom borders		

Corner Blocks

Yellow	Cut 4 (3" x 3" corner blocks)	⅛	0.125
Backing fabric		5	5

QUILTING
When the top was pieced, the outline of the pieced children was traced onto the solid background blocks with a pencil and a light table. If you don't have a light box, try using a glass-topped table or a storm-window sash with a portable lamp under it.

These outlines were then quilted by stitching over the lines twice with blue thread in free-motion machine work. The children in the pieced blocks were quilted in the ditch with white thread.

The remainder of the background of the quilt, including the border, was machine free-motion quilted with red cotton quilting thread in a continuous line of letters, numbers, words, and arabesques. I did this by eye, without marking the design in pencil first, trying to keep the density of the quilting consistent across the whole surface.

When I was tracing the children for the quilting design, I made a mistake in the orientation in one corner of the quilt: there is a break in the symmetry in one corner. Can you find it? Cotton batting.

ASSEMBLY

Sew   1 to 2 to 3
        (1,2,3) to 4
        5 to 6
        (1,2,3,4) to (5,6) to 7 to 8
        13 to 14 to 15 to 16 to 17 to 18
        9 to 10 to 11 to 12 to 19
        20 to 21
        22 to 23
        24 to 25
        (20, 21) to (22,23) to (24,25) to 26 to 27
        28 to 29 to 30

Join the five sub-units.

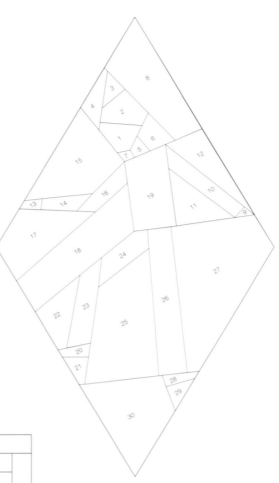

LAYOUT FOR SCRAMBLE BLOCK

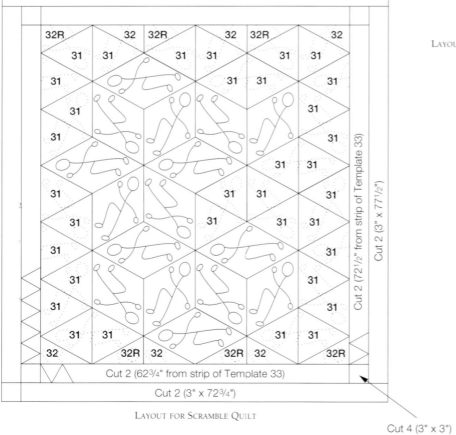

LAYOUT FOR SCRAMBLE QUILT

70

Three-PetalPosy

▪ ▪ ▪

The block for P6 is an equilateral triangle. If you begin with an equilateral triangle and number the corners 1, 2, and 3, you can lay out the arrangement below.

There is a six-way pinwheel where Corner 1's touch, and a three-way pinwheel where Corner 2's and 3's touch.

Placing Corner 2 or Corner 3 at the center of the six-way pinwheel yields two other patterns.

In designing Three-Petal Posy, I decided to demonstrate a way in which I make block quilts where the seam lines joining the blocks are hidden. I placed two petals of the flower on one edge of the block and the third petal on another edge. When two blocks are joined along Side A, the complete flower is formed. When six blocks are arranged in a hexagon with Corner 1 in the center, six complete flowers form. In searching for the unit block in the overall design, the eye's tendency is to try to place one flower in each block. Placing the center of the flower on the edge of the block hides the lines between the triangular blocks and produces an overall pattern.

In developing this kind of overall pattern, you will have to work with two or more blocks at once, so that you can see how they will match up. Begin by drawing part of the image (in this case, the posy) inside one edge of the block (Block 1). Line up another (empty) block next to Block 1 and draw the rest of the image in the second block (Block 2). On a third empty block (Block 3), trace the image from Block 1 and the rest of the image from Block 2, keeping the orientation of the blocks the way they will be assembled in the symmetry you are using. You may need to go back and adjust parts of the image in Block 1 and Block 2, so that they

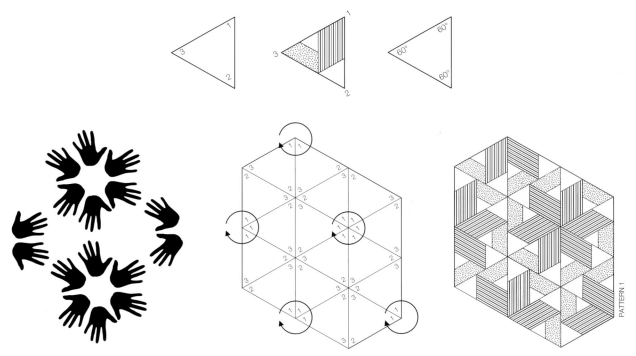

SYMMETRY NOTATION FOR P6

PATTERN 1

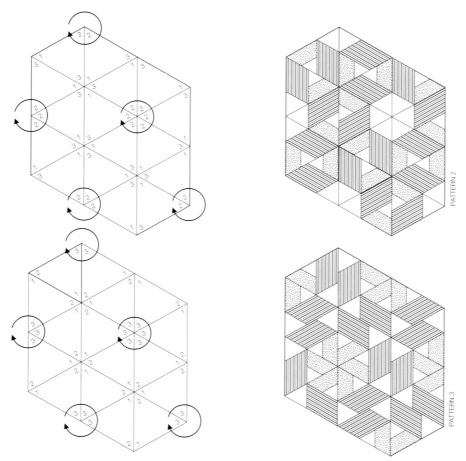

Two Additional Sets for P6 Symmetry

fit without overlapping in Block 3. Subdivide the background in Block 3 in a manner that will allow you to piece it.

Here's another example of a P6 symmetry quilt, Aquatic Rabbits, made in 1982. As you can see, one half of the rabbit is drawn on one edge of the triangle and the other half of the rabbit on the other edge. When six triangle blocks are put together, there are six whole rabbits. (As a further elaboration, this pattern was designed so that the "background" shapes would form fish with no extra pieces left over. This is similar to some of the designs of M.C. Escher.)

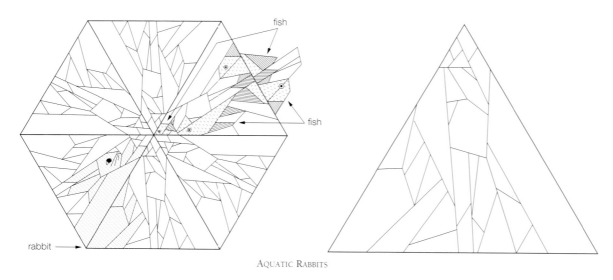

Aquatic Rabbits

TO MAKE THE QUILT ILLUSTRATED

Finished size: 52¾" x 49¼" (134 x 125 cm)
32 Three-Petal Posy Blocks: 9" equilateral triangle

| | | | | | TEMPLATE | | | | | |
Color	1	2	3	4	5	6	7	7R	Yardage	Meters
Violet 1	-	96	-	-	-	-	-	-	¾	0.75
Violet 2	96	-	-	-	-	-	-	-	½	0.5
Green	32	-	-	32	32	-	-	-	½	0.5
Rose print	96	-	-	-	-	-	-	-	½	0.5
Yellow	32	-	-	-	-	-	-	-	⅛	0.125
Blue 1	-	-	32	-	-	-	-	-	¼	0.25
Blue 2	-	-	-	-	-	32	-	-	½	0.5

Borders

A rather architectural border was built out of pieces cut from Template 7. Eight posies were assembled, then appliquéd randomly to the borders after the quilting had been done.

Assorted	-	-	-	-	-	-	34	34	1¾	1.75
Violet 2	24	-	-	-	-	-	-	-	¼	0.25

(This fabric is used wrong side up in the borders to make it a lighter color.)

Violet 3	-	24	-	-	-	-	-	-	½	0.5
Backing fabric									1⅞	1.875

QUILTING

The quilt is machine quilted with an even-feed foot, in the ditch around the posies and in parallel lines of straight and narrow programmed stitches in the border. The center of each flower is machine quilted with a variegated white-to-yellow thread in a combination of straight and fishbone stitches, as diagrammed below. Cotton batting.

- Start machine stitching where indicated.
- Straight stitch to A, pivot.
- Straight stitch to B, pivot.
- Change to fishbone stitch, stitch to C.
- Change to straight stitch, stitch to D, pivot.
- Straight stitch back to B, pivot.
- Stitch to E, pivot, repeat two times.

ASSEMBLY

Sew 1a to 2b to 1b
1c to 2c to 1d
1e to 2a to 3
1f to 4
1g to 5
1h to 6
(1a,2b,1b) to (1g,5)
(1e,2a,3) to (1f,4) to (1h,6) to (1c, 2c, 1d)
Join the sub-units.

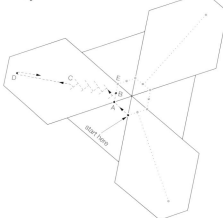

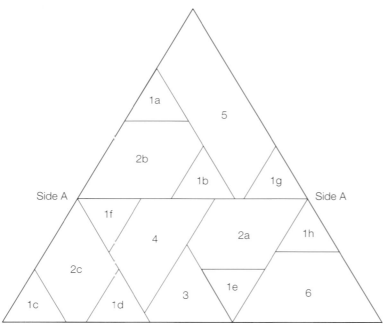

LAYOUT FOR THREE-PETAL POSY BLOCK

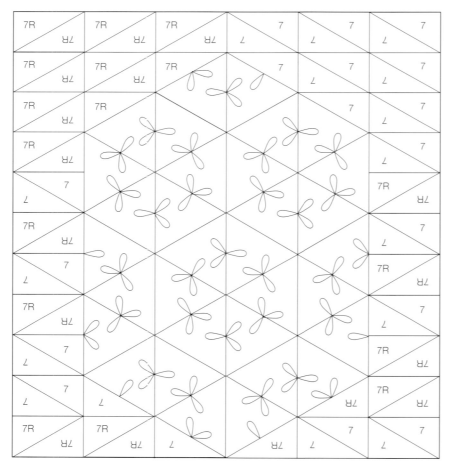

LAYOUT FOR THREE-PETAL POSY QUILT

74

CHAPTER 14
P4MM ~ FOUR MIRRORS

BullFrogs
■ ■ ■

This is the symmetry used in the great majority of traditional quilt blocks. Folding a square of paper to cut snowflakes produces the same symmetry. As a design, it is usually very stable. In "Symmetry in Traditional Blocks," we saw this type with Variable Star, Sky Rocket, Le Moyne Star, and Bird's Nest. To design an original block, begin with a right triangle for the block shape.

While the Bull Frog block I have drawn contains twenty templates, the piecing is relatively straight-forward; at only one place are there any Y-seams. Assemble the blocks in sections, as shown in the diagrams.

One of the fascinating aspects of this quilt is the manner in which the frogs appear or disappear in the eyes of the viewer. Children, for some reason, usually find the frogs before the adults do.

Drawing a pieced quilt block to represent a particular animal or plant presents a series of compromises.

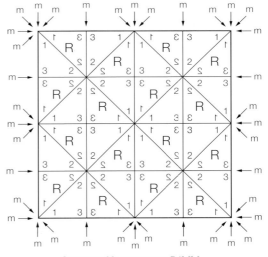

SYMMETRY NOTATION FOR P4MM

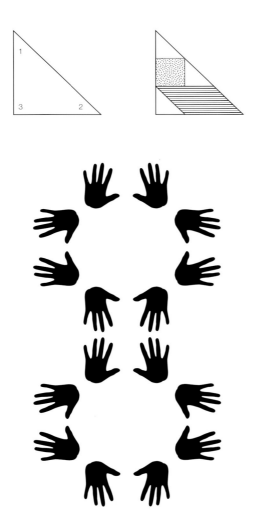

75

I usually begin to work out such a design by making a careful freehand drawing of the frog. This serves to focus me on the details, proportions, and important characteristics of the image. I chose a view, in this case from directly above the frog, in order to exploit its mirror symmetry.

Any of the symmetries with mirror lines could be used to produce a frog quilt from this viewpoint. I chose P4MM, to fit within a right-triangle block. All three edges of this triangle are mirror lines; any of them could be used as the center line of the frog. I chose to use the hypotenuse (diagonal edge) as the center of my frog.

Working from my freehand sketch, I began to fit half of a frog into the right triangle. At the same time, I began to adapt the drawing — straightening curves, moving lines, and changing angles to adapt my drawing to the piecing process. In general, I try to minimize the number of templates and Y-seams, and to keep the individual pieces of a size convenient to work with, while maintaining the essence of the frog. This process results in a series of compromises, adapting and abstracting the realistic drawing to the quilting medium.

Finally, I carefully choose a size for the block that will be appropriate both for the visual characteristics and the piecing requirements. In this case, I chose to make a 16½" block, which produces a visually interesting quilt and uses pieces of a size that most people will find convenient to work with. In other circumstances, I might have made a 12" block. Smaller than 12", the individual pieces of fabric become so small that they seem inappropriate to the medium.

Bull Frogs does not have an added border. Color changes within the quilt are sufficient to define the edge.

TO MAKE THE QUILT ILLUSTRATED
Finished size: 66½" x 66½" (168 x 168 cm)
32 Bull Frogs Blocks, 16 plain and 16 reversed: 16½" right triangle

I made this quilt from fabrics I had on hand. There are twenty different fabrics in the background and three different greens in the frogs. A table listing all of these would be unwieldy. I have therefore given you total yardage of frog green and total yardage of background fabrics. These numbers will vary somewhat, depending on how many different fabrics you choose for your quilt.

Color	TEMPLATE					Yardage	Meters
Green	Cut 16					1½	1.5
	1	1R	4	4R	5		
	5R	6	6R	11	11R		
	13	13R	15	15R			
Background	Cut 16					2	2
	2	2R	3	3R	7		
	7R	8	8R	9	9R		
	10	10R	12	12R	14		
	14R	16	16R	17	17R		
	18	18R	19	19R	20	20R	

Borders
No additional border was added to this quilt. A border is present only in that the center four blocks are colored slightly differently than the outer twelve.

Backing fabric	4	4

QUILTING

This quilt is both hand and machine quilted. With an even-feed foot, I machine stitched in the ditch around the frogs, and I stitched in parallel lines around some of the background pieces. The legs, bodies, and eyes of the frogs were quilted by hand.

ASSEMBLY

Sew   1 to 2
          3 to 4 to 5 to 6 to 7 to 8 to 9 to 10
          11 to 12 to 17
          (11,12,17) to 13 to 14 to 15 to 16
          to 18 to 19 to 20

Join the sub-units.

COMBINING BLOCKS MAKES FROGS

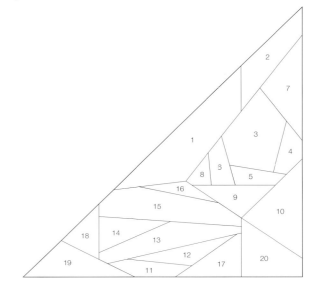

LAYOUT FOR BULL FROGS BLOCK

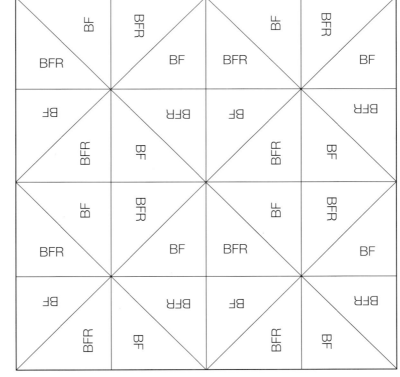

LAYOUT FOR BULL FROGS QUILT

Snow Crystal

■ ■ ■

Snowflakes are formed with this type of symmetry. I have laid it out with 30°-60°-90° triangle blocks. Twelve blocks, six plain and six mirror, fit together with the 30° point in the center to make a hexagon.

Most of the quilts in this book based on natural objects are colored in natural hues. It is certainly just as acceptable to take a form from nature and choose any colors you find pleasing. For this Snow Crystal quilt,

I've chosen red/pink, blue/green, purples, and black/white to make a vibrant small wallhanging.

As a quiltmaker, you are in charge of the color choices, limited only by the availability of the fabrics. Quilt designs based on natural images certainly do not have to be colored in a "natural" way.

Investigate Art Nouveau designs, which were often botanically very accurate but frequently colored in very unusual ways. Or look at Fauvist paintings.

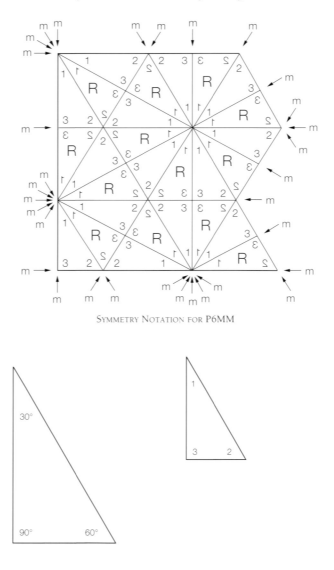

SYMMETRY NOTATION FOR P6MM

TO MAKE THE QUILT ILLUSTRATED

Finished size: 62½" x 38½" (159 x 98 cm)
24 Snow Crystal Blocks, 12 plain and 12 reversed: 15"
30°-60°-90° triangles

To simplify the piecing in the center, where twelve blocks come together, sew the blocks, leaving off Template 7 from twenty of them. Then sew the twenty blocks together in pairs. Add points to these triangles by sewing on pieces cut from Template 1.

To add variety, I used Red 1 and Red 2 fabrics wrong side up in the twelve blocks in the corners of the quilt.

	TEMPLATE								
Color	1	7	7R	10	10R	12	12R	Yardage	Meters
Red 1	12	-	-	12	12	-	-	⅜	0.375
Red 3	20	2	2	-	-	12	12	¼	0.25

	TEMPLATE						
	6	6R	8	8R	9	9R	
Red 2	12	12	-	-	-	-	¼	0.25
Pink	-	-	12	12	12	12	¼	0.25

	1	11	11R				
Blue	12	12	12		⅜	0.375
Purple	13 Cut 12		13R Cut 12		⅜	0.375
Turquoise	5 Cut 12		5R Cut 12		⅛	0.125
Teal	1 Cut 24				⅛	0.125
Green	1 Cut 24				⅛	0.125
Red violet 1	4 Cut 12		4R Cut 12		⅜	0.375
Red violet 2	3 Cut 12		3R Cut 12		¼	0.25

	TEMPLATE					
	1	2	14	14R		
Black/whites	12	12	6	6	½	0.5
Charcoals	12	12	6	6	½	0.5

Borders

Black/white checkerboard	Template 15	Cut 12	½	0.5
Cut 2 (5" x 38½") for top and bottom border				
Blue checkerboard	Template 16	Cut 2	¼	0.25
Black/white triangles	Template 17	Cut 2	⅜	0.375
	Template 17R	Cut 2		
Backing fabric			2	2

QUILTING

An overall continuous line of triangles was quilted by machine free-motion in black thread across the whole piece. Cotton batting.

ASSEMBLY

Sew 2 to 3
1a to 4
1c to 11 to 12
1d to 13
1b to 10
7 to 8
5 to 6 to 9
(2,3) to (1a,4)
(7,8) to (5,6,9) to (1b,10)
to (1c,11,12) to (1d,13) to 14

Join the sub-units.

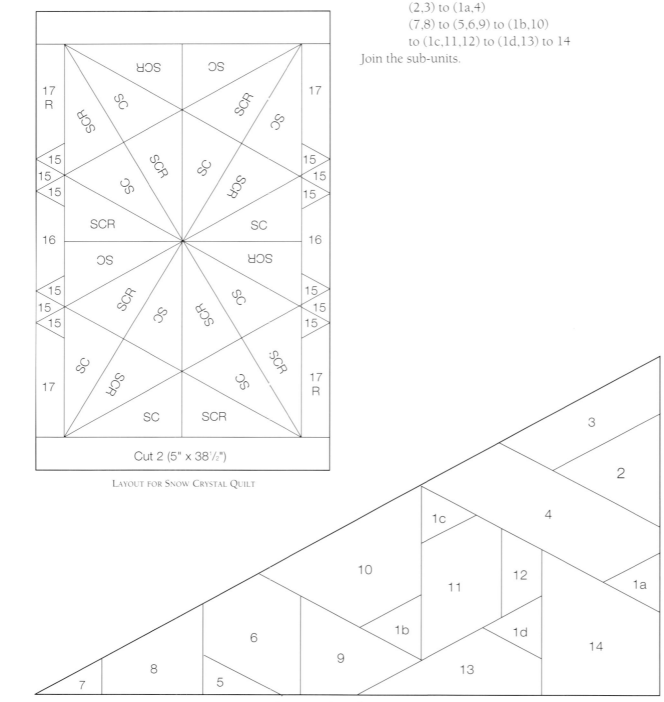

LAYOUT FOR SNOW CRYSTAL QUILT

LAYOUT FOR SNOW CRYSTAL BLOCK

Butterfly

In this symmetry I have chosen to work with a kite-shaped block, with 60°-90°-120°-90° angles. There will be a mirror line on the two long sides, and a three-way pinwheel where the 120° corners come together.

Because there is a mirror line on the long edges of this block, and because a butterfly can be viewed in mirror symmetry, the kite block works well. I have drawn one half of a butterfly in the block, placing the center line of the butterfly on one long mirror edge.

Rather than filling all of the blocks with pieced butterflies, I made some of the kite blocks of whole cloth, then quilted the butterfly image on them.

The piecing plan for the Butterfly block was worked out as described for the Bull Frog block. Although the pieces for the body of the butterfly are small, they form an important part of the design. The piecing is very straight-forward, with no Y-seams.

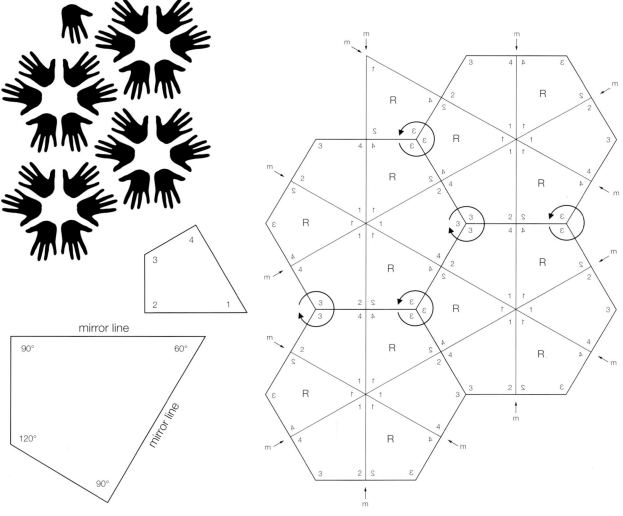

SYMMETRY NOTATION FOR P31M

TO MAKE THE QUILT ILLUSTRATED

Finished size: 63½" x 47¾" (161 x 121 cm)

24 Butterfly Blocks, 12 plain and 12 reversed: 9" 60°-90°-120°-90° kite

Color	**1**	**1R**	**8**	**8R**	**15**	**15R**			Yardage	Meters
				TEMPLATES						
Black	12	-	12	-	12	-			⅛	0.125
Brown	-	12	-	12	-	12			⅛	0.125
	3	3R	9	9R	10	10R				
Blue	12	12	12	12	12	12			⅝	0.625
	5	5R	6	6R	11	11R	12	12R		
Blue print	12	12	12	12	12	12	12	12	½	0.5
Background	2	2R	4	4R	7	7R				
	12	12	12	12	12	12			3	3
	13	13R	14	14R	16	16R				
	12	12	12	12	12	12				
	17	17R	18	18R	19	19R				
	12	12	4	2	18	18				
Backing fabric									3½	3.5

Borders

No additional border was added to this quilt.

QUILTING

The outline of the butterfly on the whole-cloth background blocks was traced with pencil using a light table. Quilting was done on the machine with an even-feed foot. A narrow blanket stitch in black thread outlines each butterfly. Those marked on the plain blocks were done in the same blanket stitch, but with off-white thread. A narrow zigzag stitch in ochre was used to echo the lines in the background print, in a series of meandering curves. Cotton batting.

ASSEMBLY

Sew
    1 to 2
    8 to 9
    15 to 16
    3 to 4 to 5 to 6 to 7 to (1,2) to (8,9)
    10 to 11 to 12 to 13 to 14 to 17 to (15,16)

Join the sub-units.

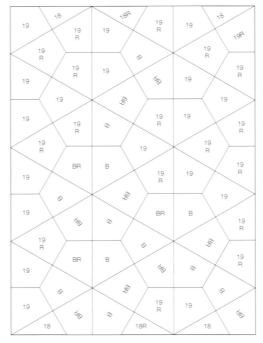

LAYOUT FOR BUTTERFLY QUILT

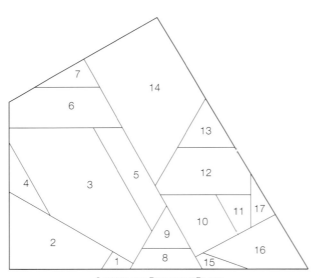

LAYOUT FOR BUTTERFLY BLOCK

Trillium

■ ■ ■

Like P6 in Chapter 13, P3M1 fits together with equilateral triangle blocks. Unlike P6, this symmetry has mirrors. Each intersection at the corners of the blocks is a three-way pinwheel of a mirrored pair of blocks.

The geometry of this symmetry is perfect to make a trillium. The flower has three even petals, sepals, and a three-part leaf. Taking advantage of the mirrors, I am able to draw a block with a half-petal, a half-sepal, and a half-leaf; in completing the symmetry I have the complete plant.

By considering any geometry present in a plant while you choose a block shape and symmetry pattern for a possible quilt, you can give unity to the final design. The equilateral triangle block and P3M1 sym-

metry reflect the structure of the trillium itself. Careful looking at an individual plant may help you find a symmetry that you did not see at first glance.

QUILTING

Several different types of free-motion machine quilting were used on this piece. The outer border was quilted with a straight stitch in navy thread, in a free arabesque pattern. The center of the flowers was held down with white stitching in wavy lines. The blue fabric pieces were quilted with variegated metallic thread.

The veins in the leaves were added by free-motion stitching in dark green. The remainder of the center of the quilt is stitched by free-motion in a wavy pattern, but with the machine set for a medium zigzag rather than a straight stitch. Dark red thread was used in the outer part, orange in the next row, and yellow-orange in the center. Cotton batting.

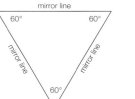

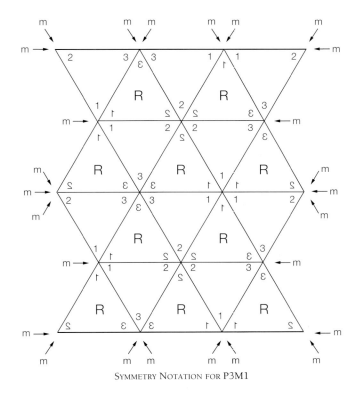

SYMMETRY NOTATION FOR P3M1

83

TO MAKE THE QUILT AS ILLUSTRATED

Finished size: 64" x 55" (163 x 140 cm)
54 Trillium Blocks, 27 plain and 27 reversed: 9⅛" equilateral triangle

To give some variety of shading to the leaves and petals and more interest to the quilt surface, I used slightly different fabrics in the plain blocks and the mirror blocks. If you choose that option, cut 27 petals (Template 1) for the plain blocks from one white fabric, and 27 petals (Template 1R) for the mirror blocks from another white fabric. Similarly, I used two greens, two reds, and two blues. You will have to adjust the yardage below accordingly.

Color	1	1R	2	2R	3	4	4R	Yardage	Meters
White	27	27	-	-	-	-	-	⅜	0.375
Red	-	-	27	27	-	-	-	⅜	0.375
Multi print	-	-	-	-	54	-	-	⅛	0.125
Black print	-	-	-	-	-	27	27	¾	0.75
	5	5R	6	6R	7	7R			
Pale green	27	27	-	-	-	-		⅛	0.125
Green	-	-	27	27	-	-		1⅝	1.625
Blue	-	-	-	-	27	27		¾	0.75
	8	8R							
Teal	27	27						½	0.25

Borders

				Yardage	Meters
Multi print	**Template 9**	Cut 18		⅜	0.375
Red	**Template 3**	Cut 24		⅛	0.125
Black	**Template 10**	Cut 12		¼	0.25
Blue	**Template 11**	Cut 6		¾	0.75
Backing fabric				3½	3.5

ASSEMBLY

Sew   1 to 2
         3 to 4
         6 to 7 to 8
         (3,4) to 5 to (1,2)
Join the sub-units.

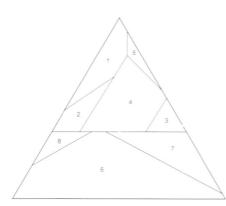

LAYOUT FOR TRILLIUM BLOCK

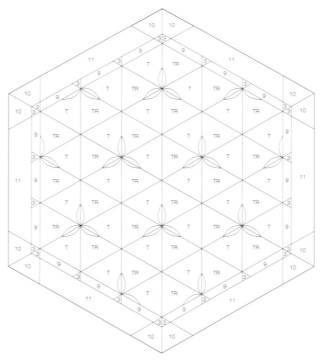

LAYOUT FOR TRILLIUM QUILT

Playing with Part 2 Blocks

Some of the blocks from the Part 2 quilts will fit into some of the other symmetries. For example, here is the Scramble (Chapter 12) diamond used in P2 symmetry.

RIGHT TRIANGULAR FROG BLOCK IN P4GM SYMMETRY

SCRAMBLE DIAMOND BLOCK IN P2 SYMMETRY

Four-way pinwheels can be constructed from right triangle blocks if you put the right angle at the center of the pinwheel. Bull Frogs is arranged this way here, in P4GM symmetry.

It is interesting to explore which of these basic block shapes — Baby Block Diamonds, Right Triangles, Equilateral Triangles, 30°-60°-90° Triangles, and 60° Kites — will fit together in which of the symmetries. Now investigate which other possible block shapes you could use.

The study of block shapes in terms useful to pieced quilts can proceed from a study of the mathematical concept of tessellation: finding shapes that, when reproduced many times, will fit together to cover a surface, with no holes and no overlaps. It is a subject which I have found fascinating, and on which I expect to do some more work. You may well find that this book has inspired you to do so, too.

WHERE DO WE GO FROM HERE?

Illustrated below are the 22 different symmetrical patterns we've made from the square and rectangular blocks in Part 1.

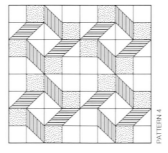

PATTERN 4

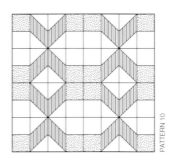

PATTERN 10

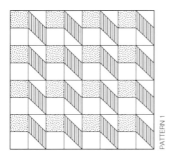

PATTERN 1

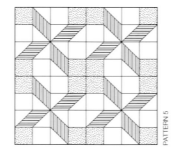

PATTERN 5

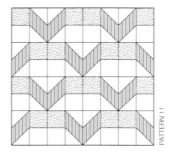

PATTERN 11

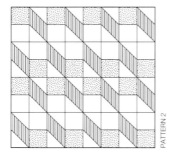

PATTERN 2

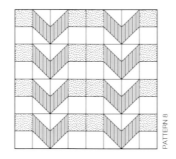

PATTERN 8

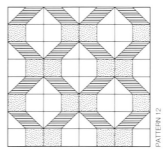

PATTERN 12

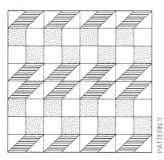

PATTERN 3

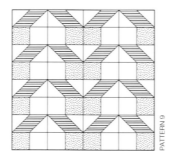

PATTERN 9

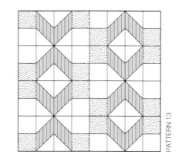

PATTERN 13

22 SYMMETRY PATTERNS FROM A SQUARE ASYMMETRICAL BLOCK

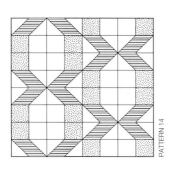

PATTERN 14

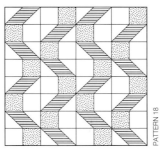

PATTERN 18

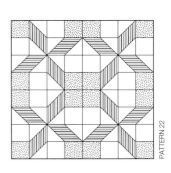

PATTERN 22

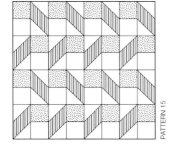

PATTERN 15

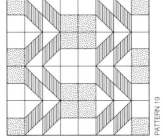

PATTERN 19

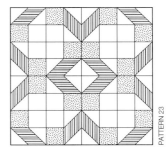

PATTERN 23

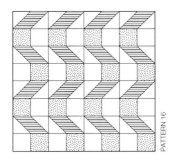

PATTERN 16

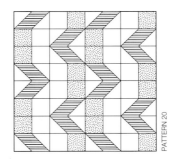

PATTERN 20

PATTERN 24

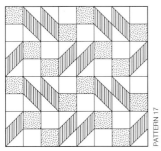

PATTERN 17

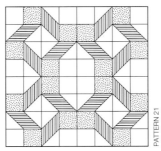

PATTERN 21

22 SYMMETRY PATTERNS FROM A SQUARE ASYMMETRICAL BLOCK (CONT.)

With rectangular blocks in pinwheel symmetries, there are these variations:

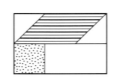

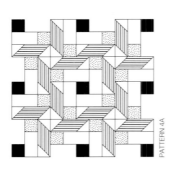
PATTERN 4A

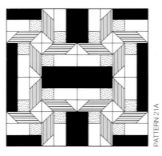
PATTERN 21A

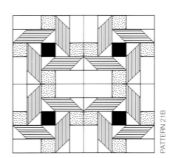
PATTERN 21B

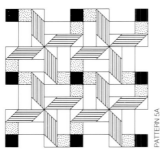
PATTERN 5A

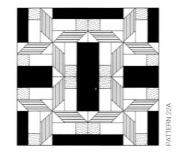
PATTERN 22A

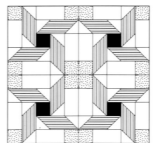
PATTERN 22B

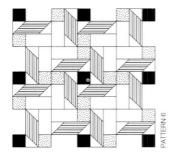
PATTERN 6

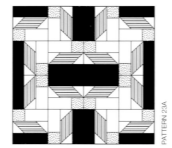
PATTERN 23A

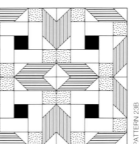
PATTERN 23B

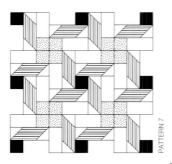
PATTERN 7

PATTERN 24A

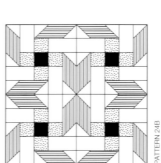
PATTERN 24B

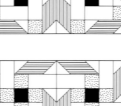

12 PINWHEEL PATTERNS FROM A RECTANGULAR ASYMMETRICAL BLOCK

You can see some of the advantages of beginning with an asymmetrical block.

Beyond a rigid approach to symmetry, here are some other approaches you may enjoy exploring.

Begin a symmetry pattern in one corner of a quilt, then dissolve it in a random way. In the next illustration, I have begun with a section of P2 symmetry, the second pattern of the square set, in the upper left. Then I

DISSOLVING A SYMMETRY

BORDERING ONE SYMMETRY WITH ANOTHER

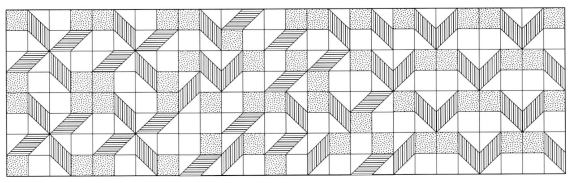

TRANSFORMING ONE SYMMETRY INTO ANOTHER

turned the blocks in the bottom right out of P2 symmetry in a random way. You can see the order at the upper left, and the progressive disorder as the blocks move down and to the right.

Start with one symmetry pattern on one side of a quilt and blend it into another symmetry pattern on the other side. Here I have begun with P4 symmetry (the sixth pattern of the square set) at the left side of the quilt, then drawn an area of CM, the eleventh pattern, at the right side of the same quilt. The area in between is filled with some randomly turned blocks, to unite one side with the other.

Combine two or more symmetries in the same quilt. Here, sixteen blocks in P4GM are surrounded by a border of PM. The center sixteen blocks of this quilt are P4

symmetry, the eleventh pattern of the first set. The outer forty-eight blocks are arranged in PM symmetry, the ninth pattern turned on its side. Coloring both the inner blocks and the outer PM set the same way would make a very subtle border. Or, by coloring the inner sixteen P4 blocks in one scheme and the outer blocks in another, you can make a dramatically different quilt.

As I indicated in the introduction, I have allowed myself some freedom in inventing coloring schemes for the seventeen basic quilts in the book. In Viola and Musical Notation, each block in the quilt is colored in exactly the same way. The other quilts show a variety of different ways to vary the colors in a quilt. It is certainly also possible to make each block in a symmetry quilt in a different color scheme. *You* are the artist. *You* decide.

VIOLA QUILT — CHAPTER 1

MUSICAL NOTATION QUILT — CHAPTER 2

PAINTED DAISIES QUILT — CHAPTER 3

LILIES QUILT — CHAPTER 4

POPPIES QUILT — CHAPTER 5

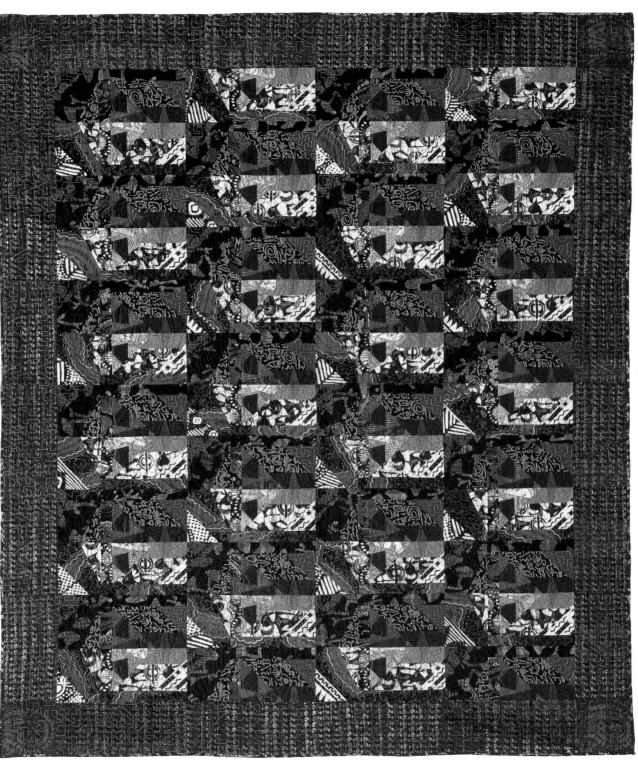

LIGHTNING STRIKE QUILT — CHAPTER 7

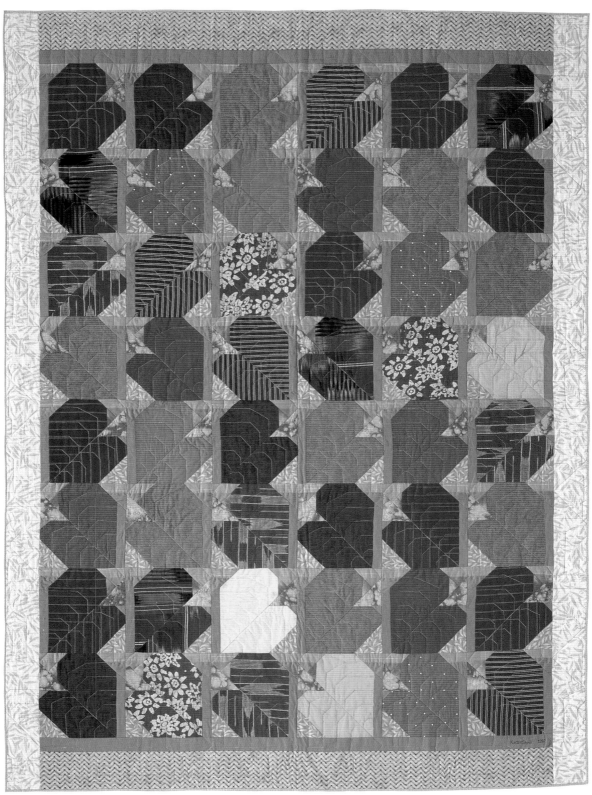

KATSURA LEAVES QUILT — CHAPTER 8

DECO MOON QUILT — CHAPTER 9

Spinning Rings Quilt — Chapter 11

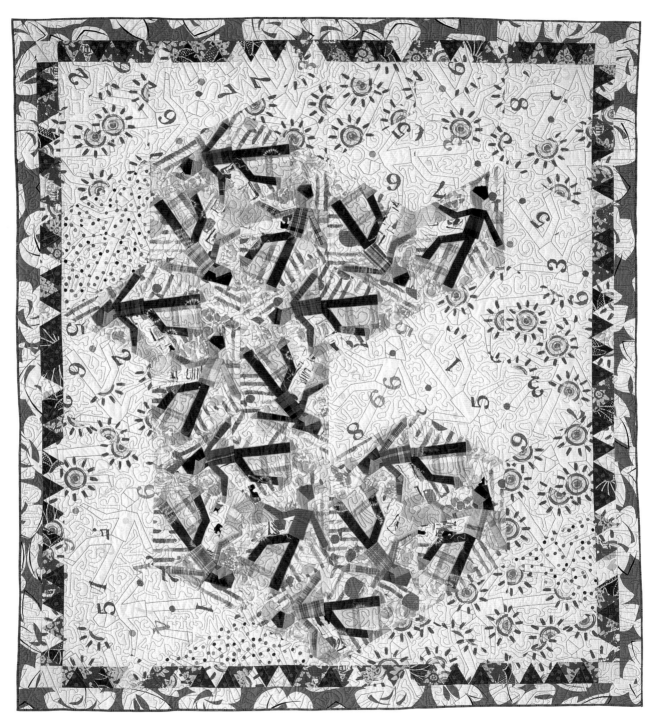

SCRAMBLE QUILT — CHAPTER 12

Three-Petal Posy Quilt — Chapter 13

BULL FROGS QUILT — CHAPTER 14

SNOW CRYSTAL QUILT — CHAPTER 15

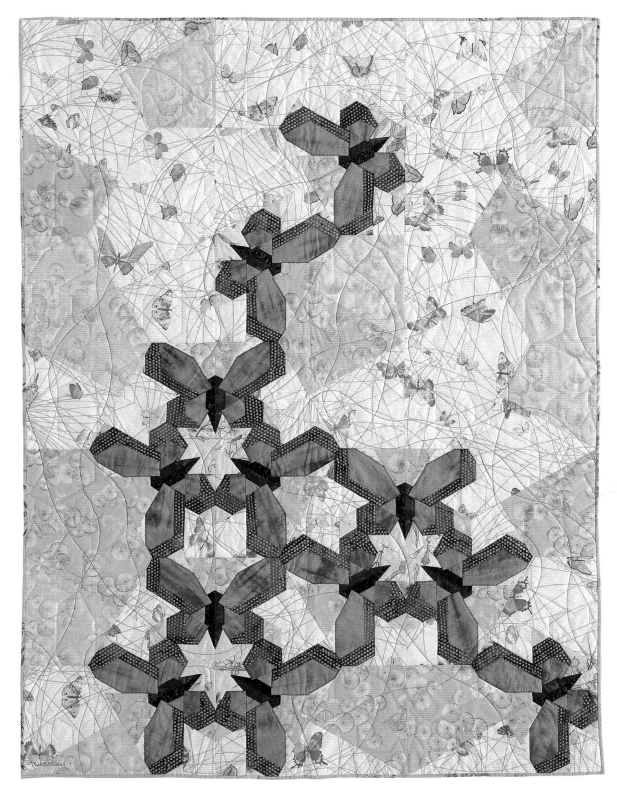

BUTTERFLY QUILT — CHAPTER 16

TRILLIUM QUILT — CHAPTER 17

USING SYMMETRY IN THE SCHOOLS

Nancy Crasco, a fine contemporary quiltmaker and teacher, has been using symmetry as part of her curriculum in Ottoson Junior High School in Arlington, Massachusetts. In their math courses, the students are gradually introduced to simple concepts in geometry, perimeter, and volume, as well as bilateral symmetry.

In the seventh grade, Nancy, a graduate of Rhode Island School of Design, begins to introduce the concepts of tessellation and patterns. Students choose a shape and look for it in their everyday surroundings. They look at tiles and at regular shapes, and at how they are used together. As a final project, each student makes a tessellation. Then, using recycled pieces of greeting cards or wallpaper, each student invents another design to be placed on top of the symmetry. In a verbal presentation before the class, each describes the choice of symmetry and the finished project.

In the eighth grade, Nancy introduces the symmetry patterns we've looked at in Part 1. She says that the students get very excited, because it's usually a learning process for their teachers as well and everyone starts off on the same footing. With a co-operative learning approach, the students are placed in groups of four and assigned one of the simpler symmetries to study. It will be their responsibility to teach "their" symmetry to the rest of the class. One of the real benefits of this process is that it is not always the "brightest" students who are the quickest to catch on. Spatial giftedness is usually not rewarded in the academic environment of a school. This is a chance for students with special spatial abilities to shine. Each student selects one symmetry, designs a pattern, and enlarges it for a final project. It is also an opportunity to relate mathematical concepts to art and design, and it can make math exciting in a whole new way. Her students are introduced to the notation system we have used in this book and understand what a crystallographer does. Nancy also notes that the exercise really improves the students' measuring skills.

As I hope I've demonstrated in this book, a systematic approach to symmetry is a wonderful aid in making this kind of design readily accessible to quiltmakers. It seems certainly to be extremely useful as well in many other fine and applied art curricula and as a means of relating the world of mathematics to the world of art.

Conclusion

I find symmetry every bit as exciting an idea now as I did ten years ago. Like the reverberant patterning in my 1991 book, *Pattern on Pattern*, it is part of the vocabulary of design. Understanding these basic concepts will enable you to make them work for you in your designing, using as much or as little of each as is required by a particular project. It opens the design process up to more possibilities, in the same way that increasing your vocabulary of words will expand your options as a writer.

Quiltmaking is a homespun American tradition that can combine all of the design elements of fine art if you choose to use them. At the same time, quilts can be made on a much less self-conscious level, serving as warm and cozy bedcovers or wall decorations. They can be as improvisational or as precisely planned as you choose to make them.

Within all these options, I hope that this study of symmetry patterns and asymmetrical blocks will help to open your horizons and thereby allow you to express yourself with creative design.

BIBLIOGRAPHY

General

Buerger, Martin. *Elementary Crystallography: An Introduction to the Fundamental Geometric Features of Crystals.* Cambridge: The MIT Press, 1978.

Grunbaum, Branko, and G. C. Shephard. *Tiling and Patterns.* New York: W. H. Freeman, 1987.

McDowell, Ruth B. *Pattern on Pattern.* Gualala, Calif.: The Quilt Digest Press, 1991.

Stevens, Peter S. *Handbook of Regular Patterns: An Introduction to Symmetry in Two Dimensions.* Cambridge: The MIT Press, 1981.

Illustrations of various symmetry patterns

Bentley, W. A., and W. J. Humphreys. *Snow Crystals.* New York: Dover Publications, 1931.

Escher, M. C. Any book of his drawings

Verneuil, M. P. *Floral Patterns: 120 Full Color Designs in the Art Nouveau Style.* New York: Dover Publications, 1981.

There are many other picture books in which you can find examples of symmetry patterns.

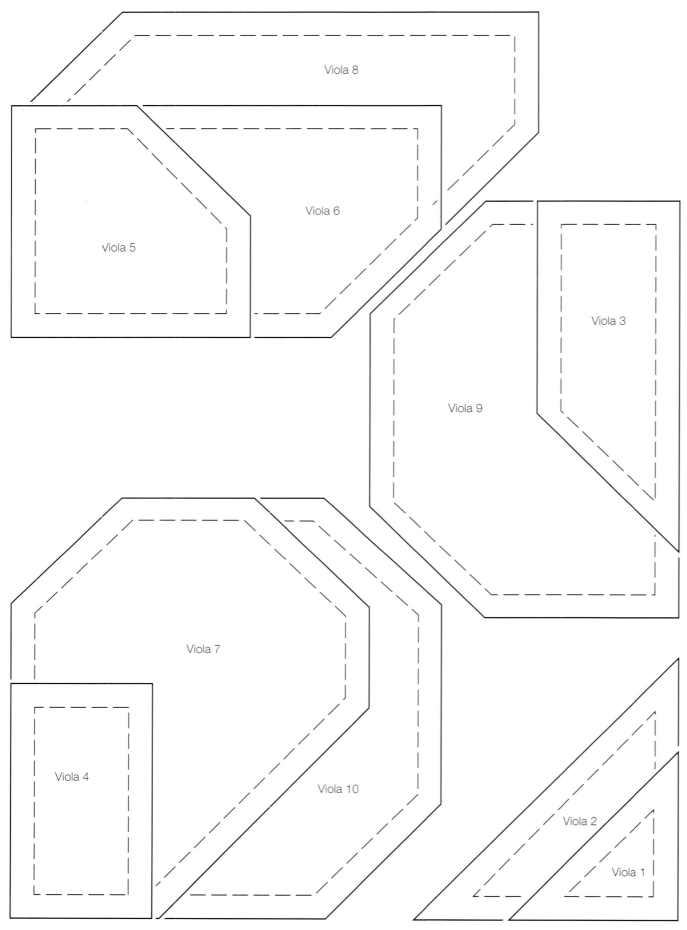

Viola 8

Viola 6

viola 5

Viola 3

Viola 9

Viola 7

Viola 4

Viola 10

Viola 2

Viola 1

110

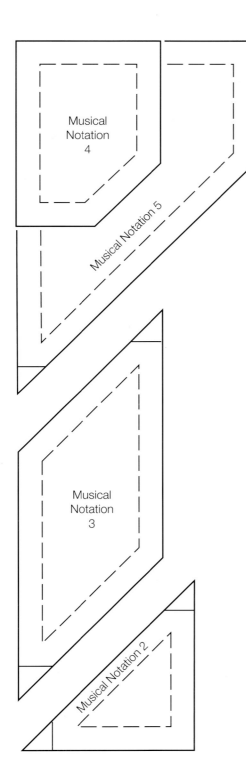

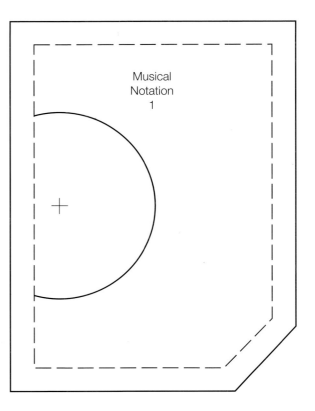

Musical Notation 4

Musical Notation 5

Musical Notation 3

Musical Notation 2

Musical Notation 1

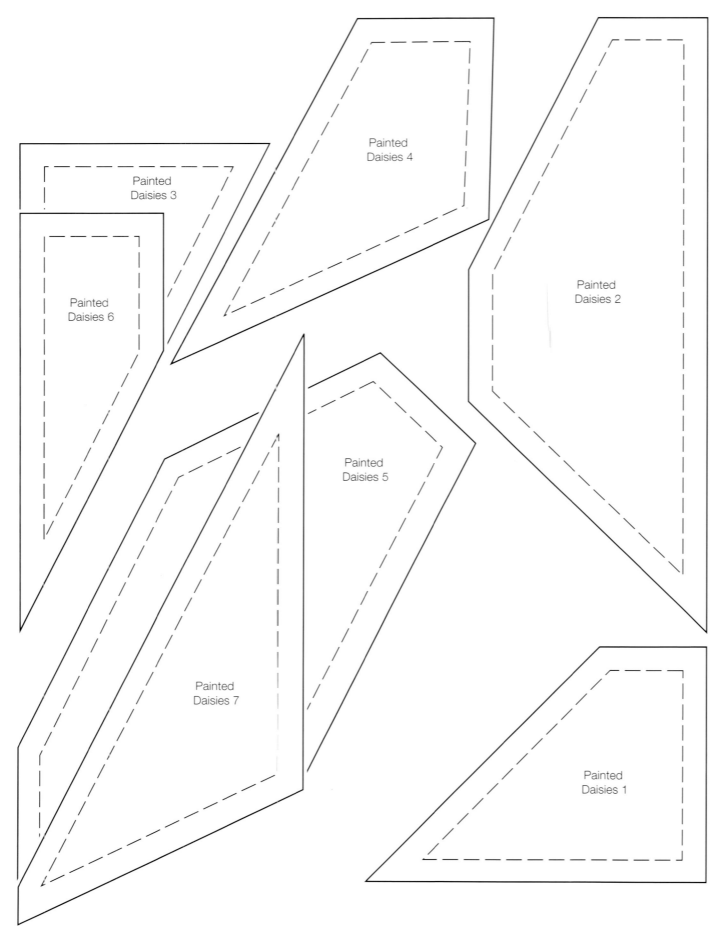

Painted
Daisies 4

Painted
Daisies 2

Painted
Daisies 3

Painted
Daisies 6

Painted
Daisies 5

Painted
Daisies 7

Painted
Daisies 1

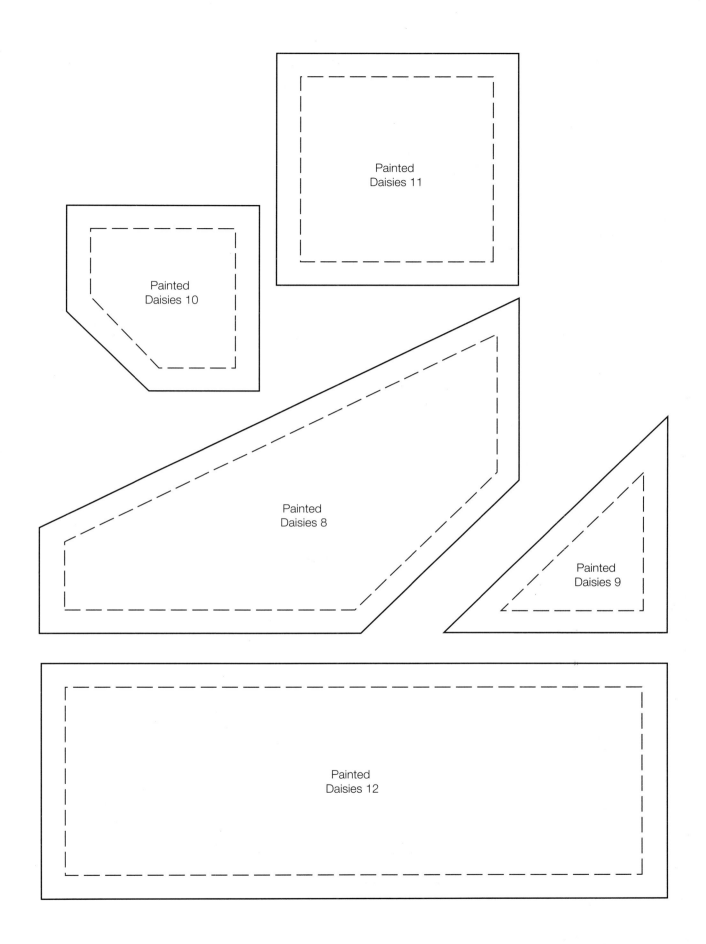

Painted
Daisies 11

Painted
Daisies 10

Painted
Daisies 8

Painted
Daisies 9

Painted
Daisies 12

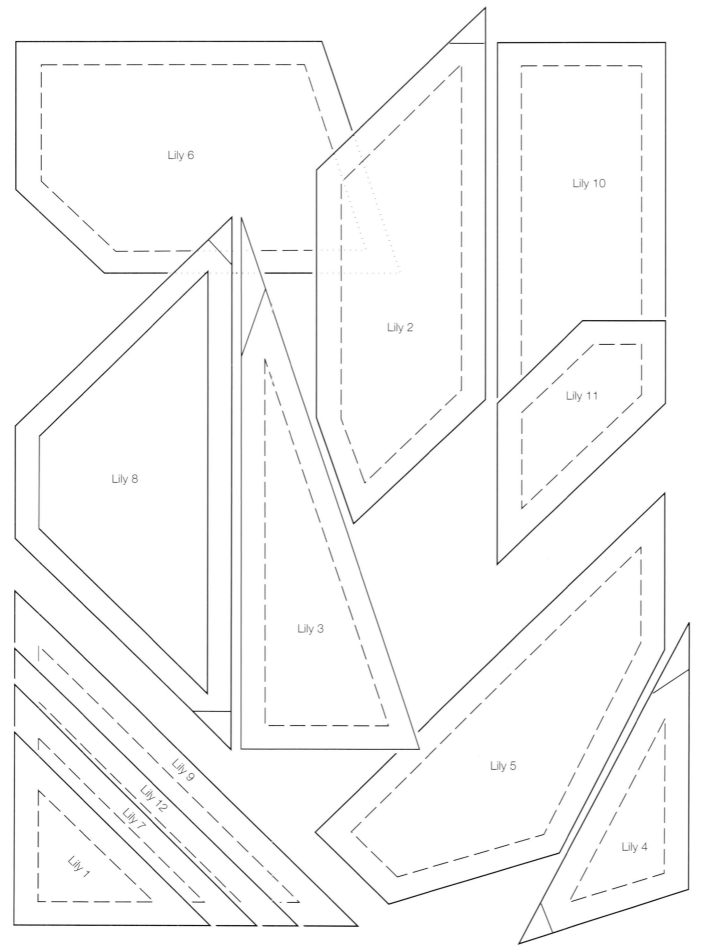

Lily 6

Lily 10

Lily 2

Lily 11

Lily 8

Lily 3

Lily 5

Lily 9

Lily 12

Lily 7

Lily 1

Lily 4

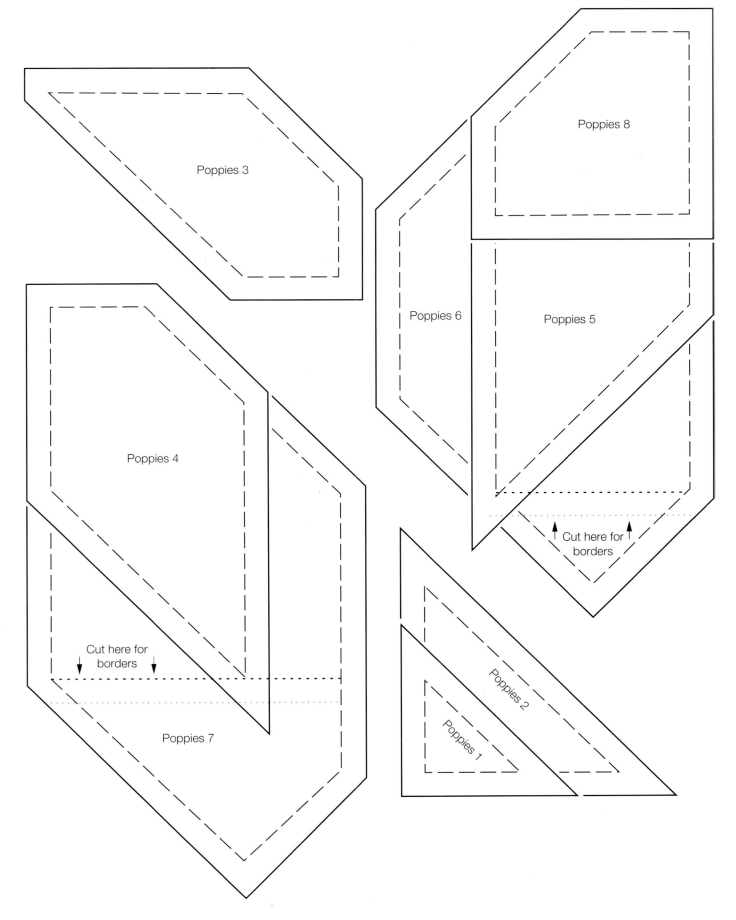

Poppies 3

Poppies 8

Poppies 6

Poppies 5

Poppies 4

Cut here for borders

Poppies 7

Cut here for borders

Poppies 2

Poppies 1

115

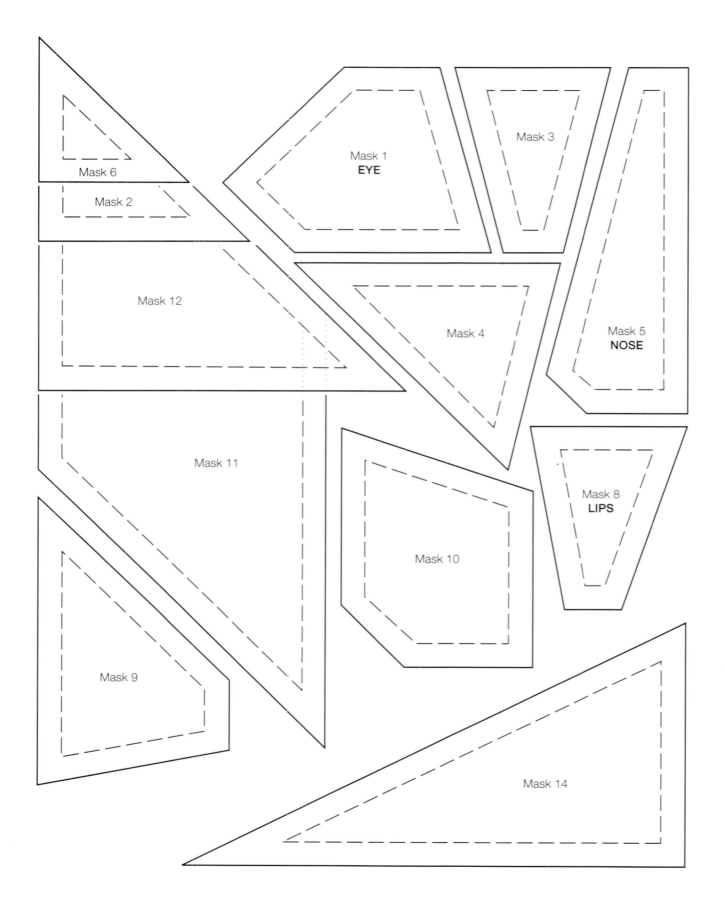

Mask 6

Mask 2

Mask 1
EYE

Mask 3

Mask 12

Mask 4

Mask 5
NOSE

Mask 11

Mask 8
LIPS

Mask 10

Mask 9

Mask 14

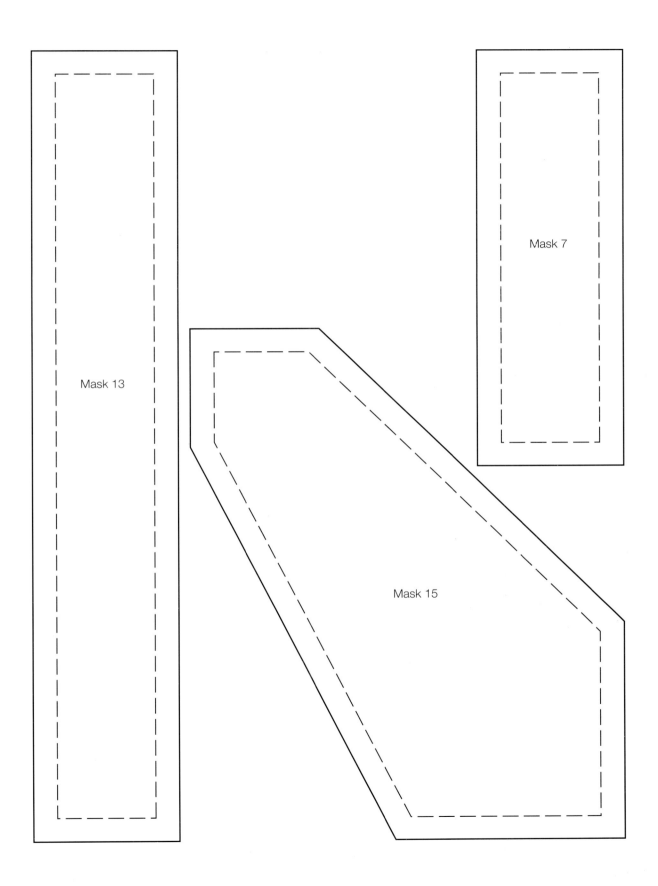

Mask 13

Mask 7

Mask 15

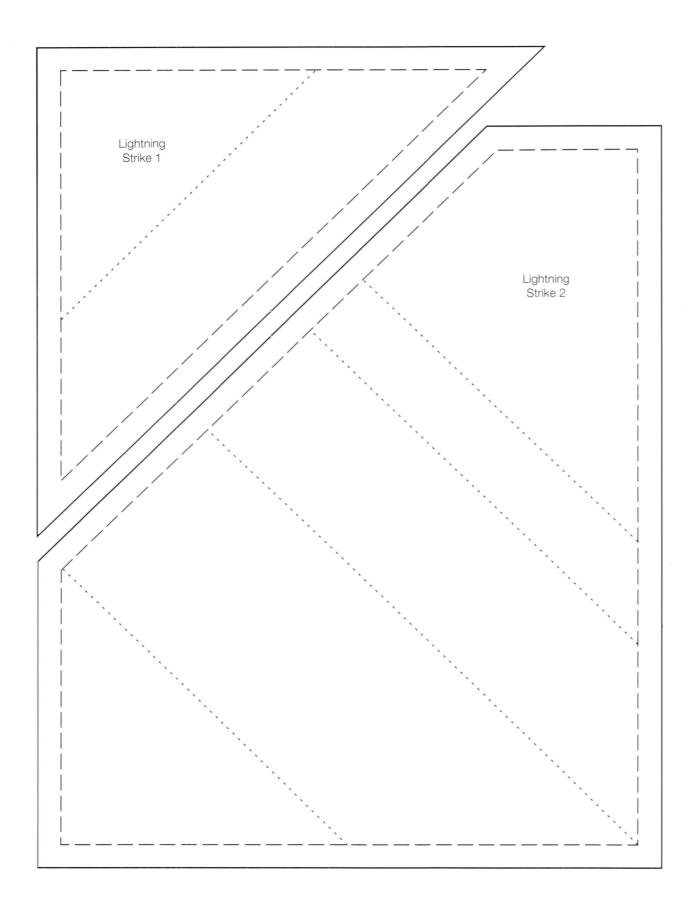

Lightning
Strike 1

Lightning
Strike 2

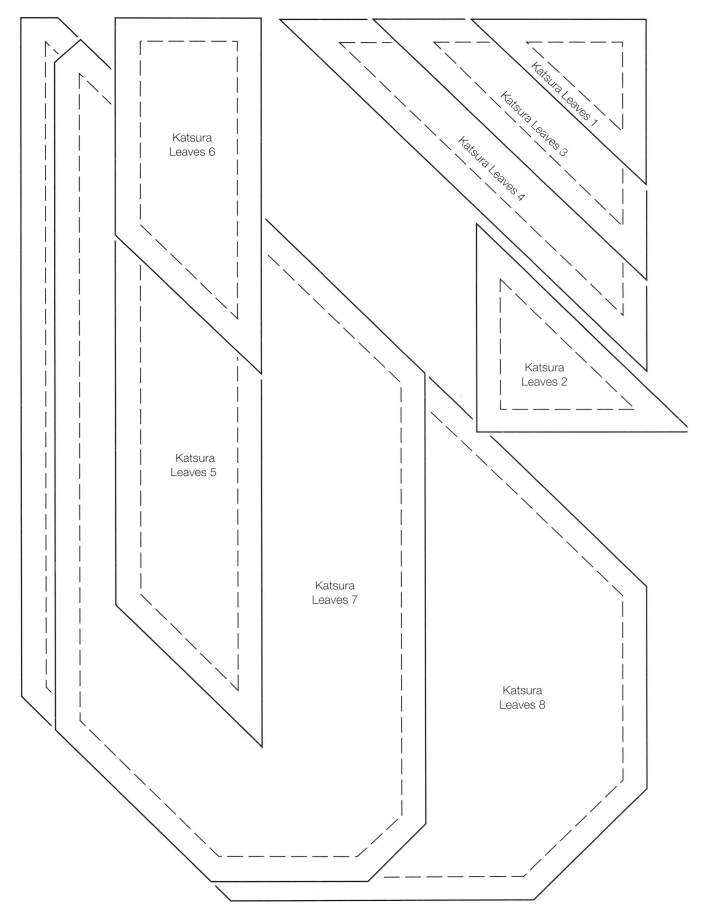

Katsura Leaves 1

Katsura Leaves 3

Katsura Leaves 4

Katsura
Leaves 6

Katsura
Leaves 2

Katsura
Leaves 5

Katsura
Leaves 7

Katsura
Leaves 8

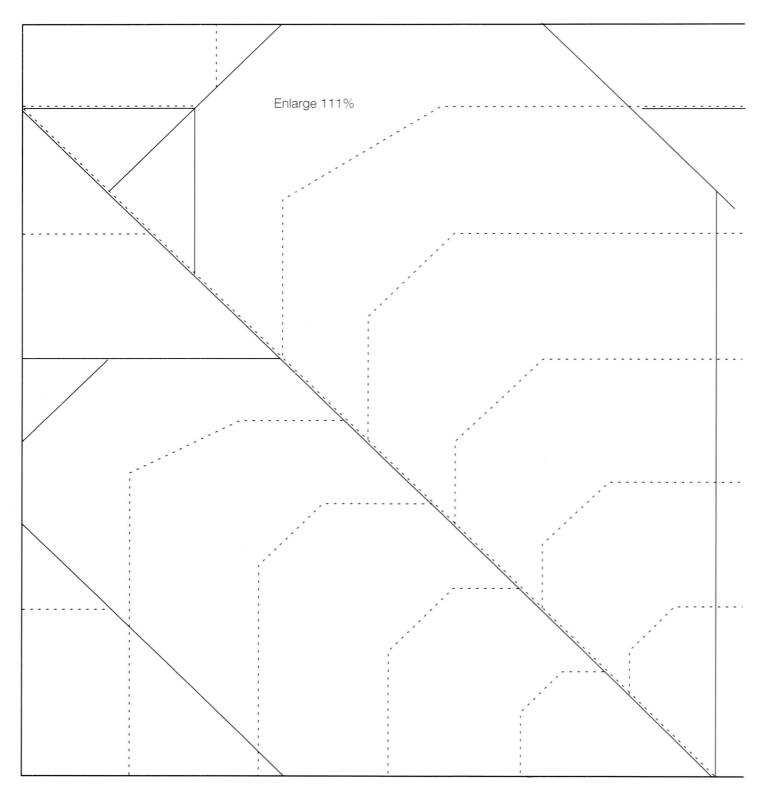

Enlarge 111%

Quilting diagram for Katsura Leaves

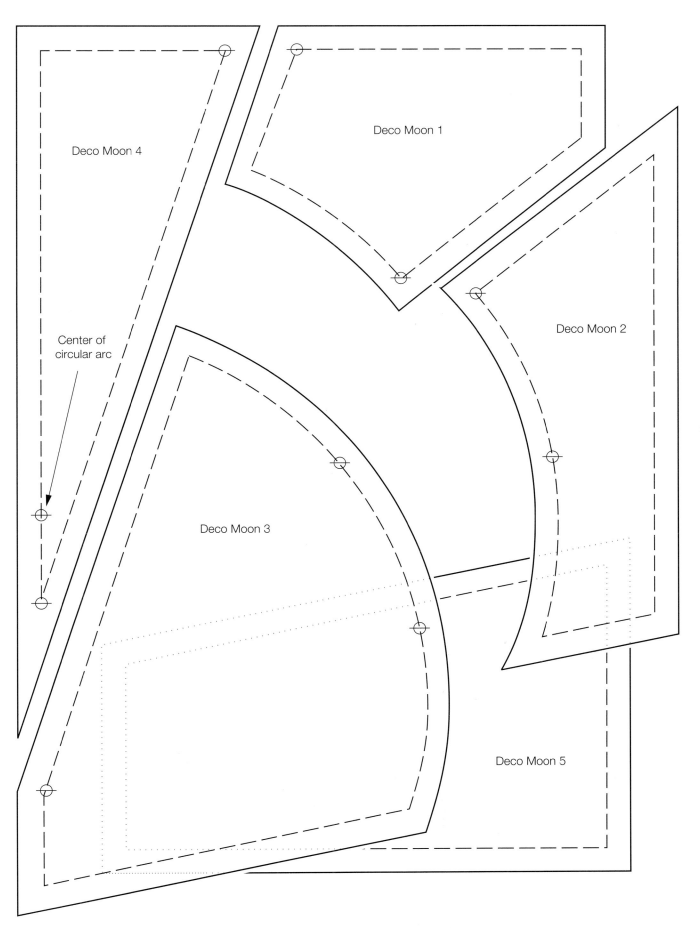

Deco Moon 4

Deco Moon 1

Deco Moon 2

Center of
circular arc

Deco Moon 3

Deco Moon 5

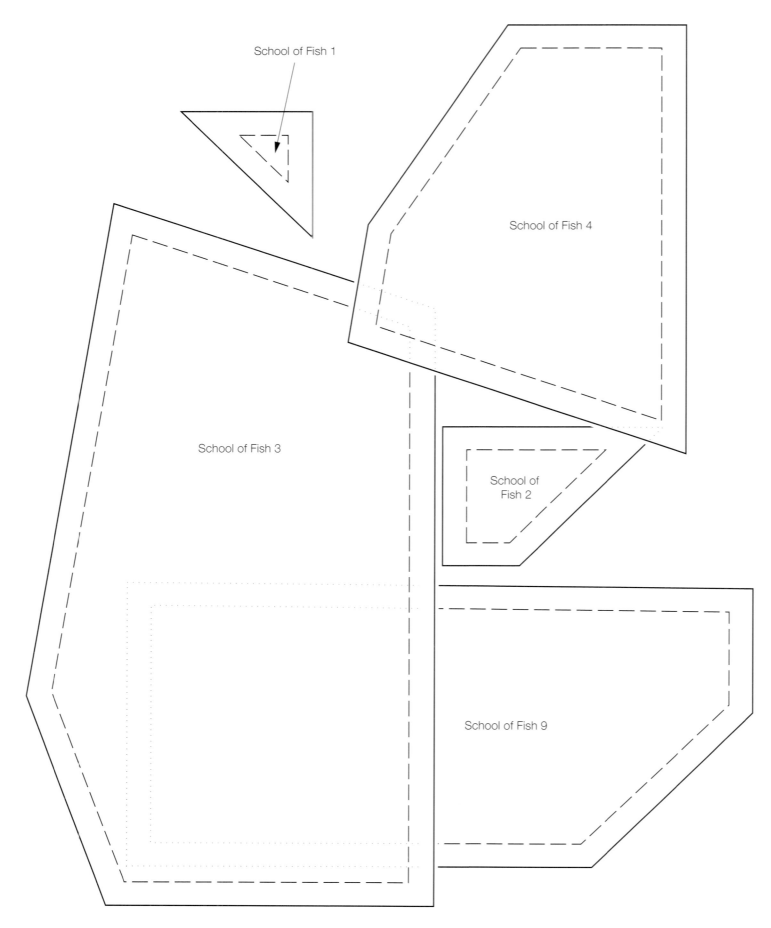

School of Fish 1

School of Fish 4

School of Fish 3

School of Fish 2

School of Fish 9

122

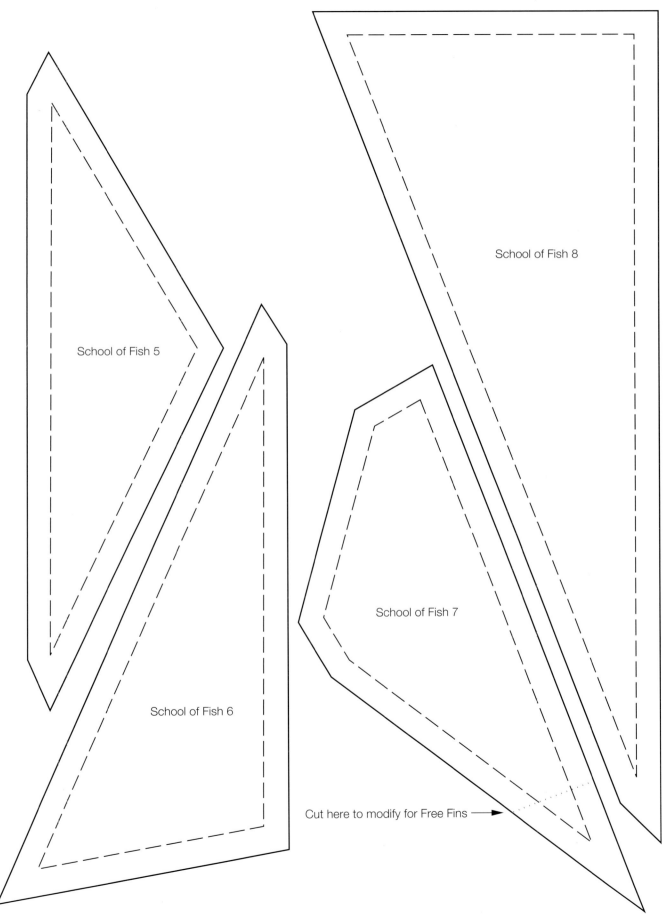

School of Fish 5

School of Fish 6

School of Fish 8

School of Fish 7

Cut here to modify for Free Fins ⟶

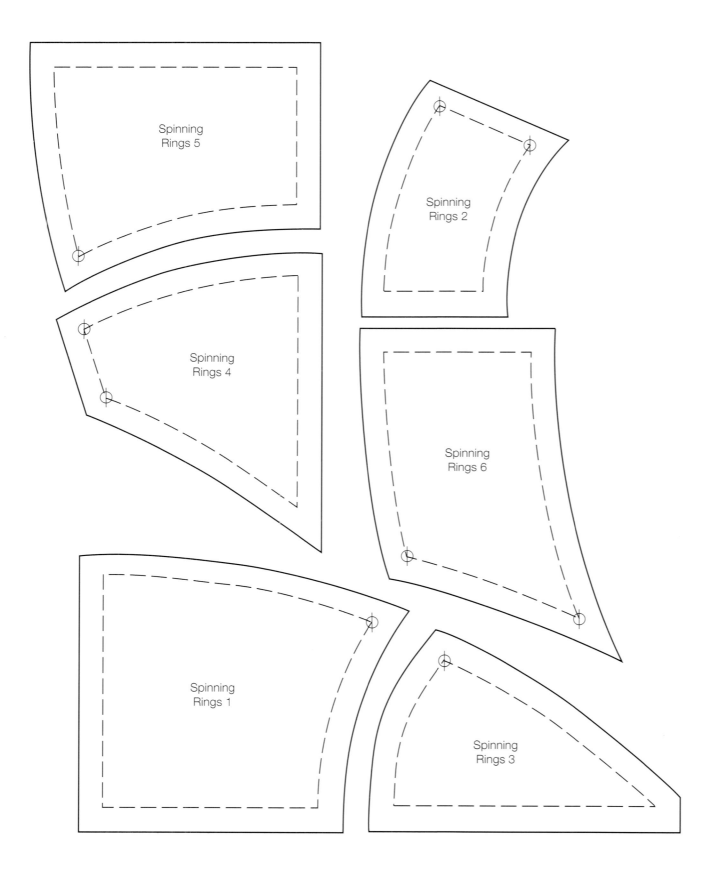

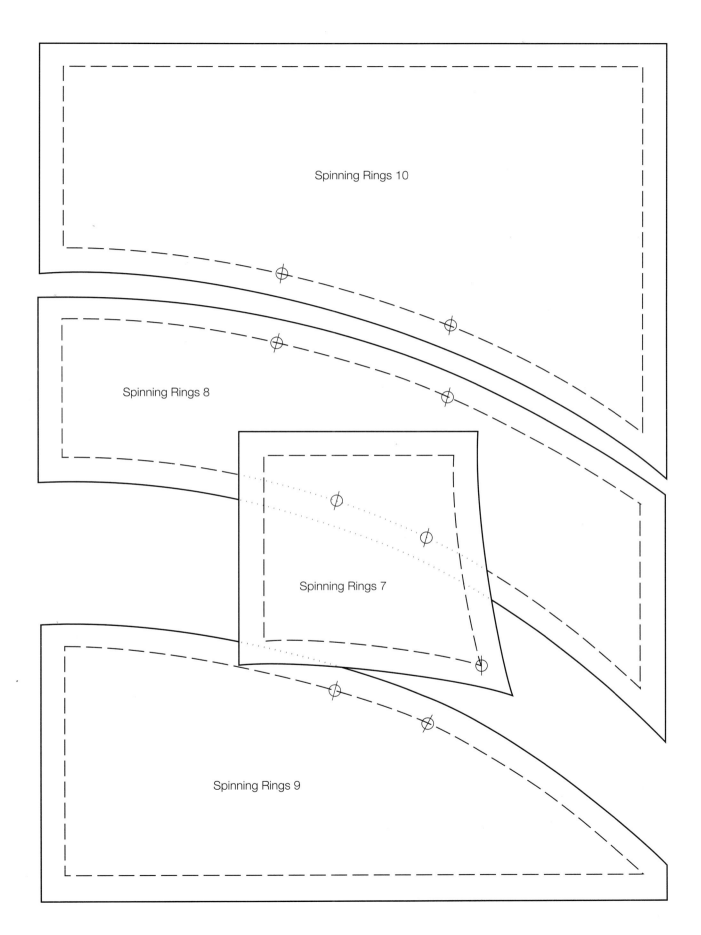

Spinning Rings 10

Spinning Rings 8

Spinning Rings 7

Spinning Rings 9

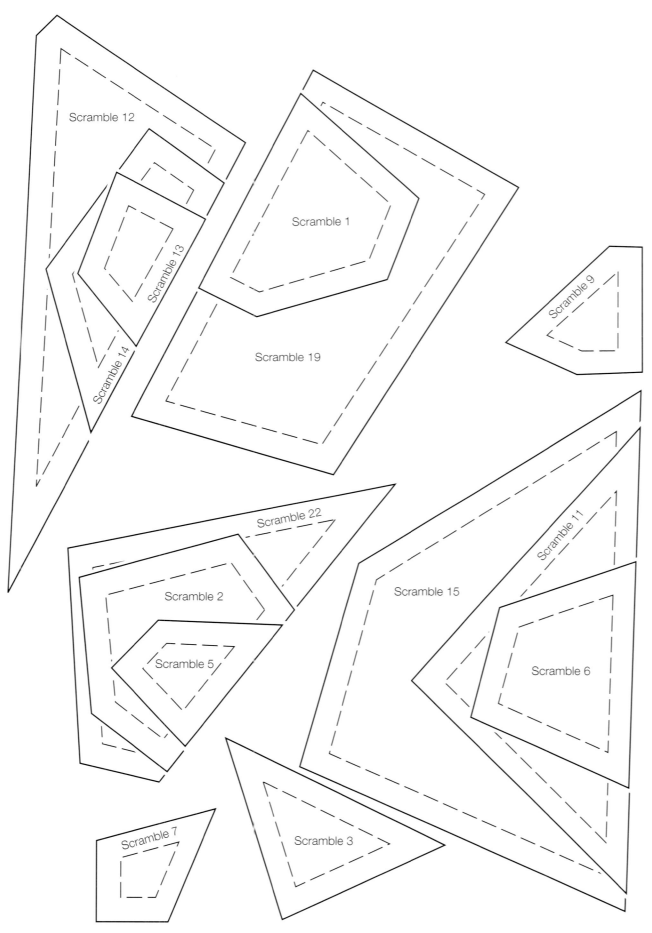

Scramble 12

Scramble 13

Scramble 14

Scramble 1

Scramble 19

Scramble 9

Scramble 22

Scramble 2

Scramble 5

Scramble 11

Scramble 15

Scramble 6

Scramble 7

Scramble 3

126

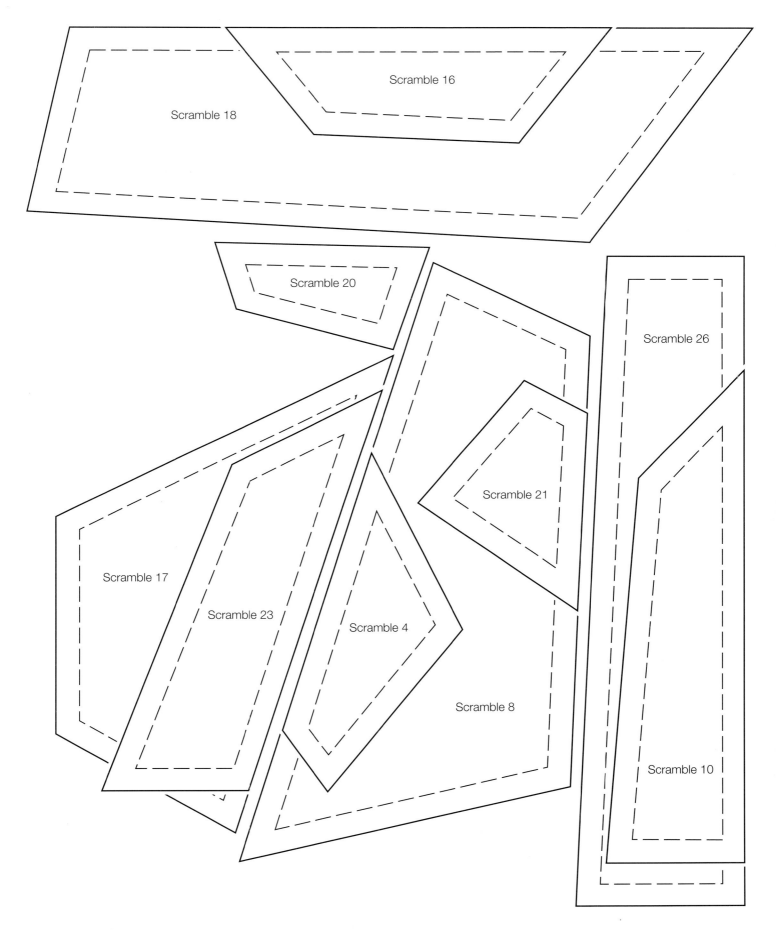

Scramble 16

Scramble 18

Scramble 20

Scramble 26

Scramble 21

Scramble 17

Scramble 23

Scramble 4

Scramble 8

Scramble 10

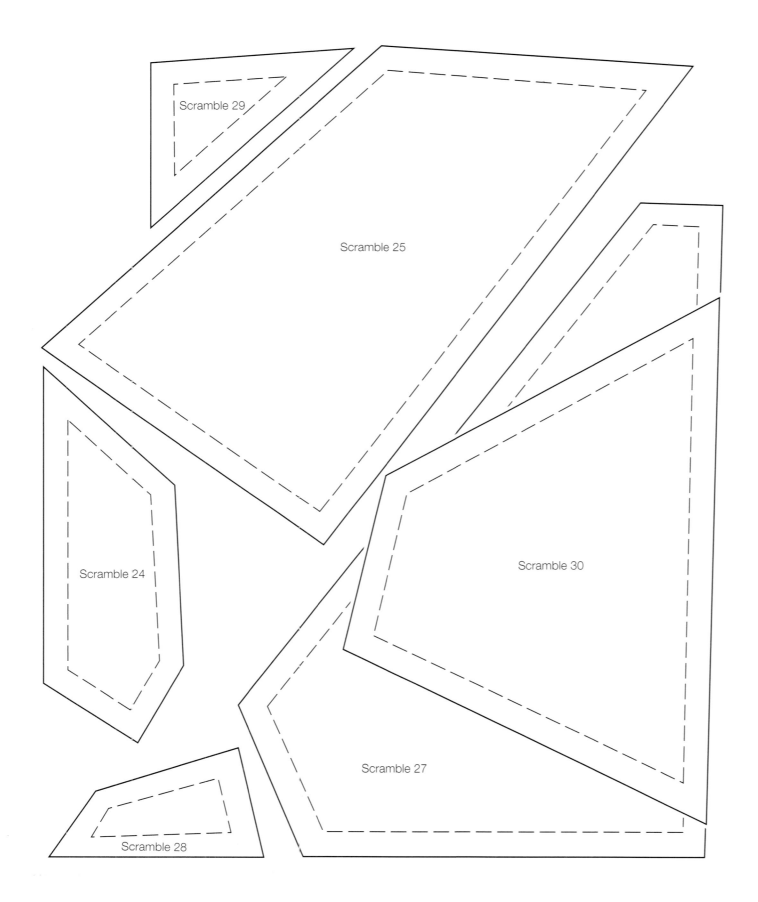

Scramble 29

Scramble 25

Scramble 24

Scramble 30

Scramble 27

Scramble 28

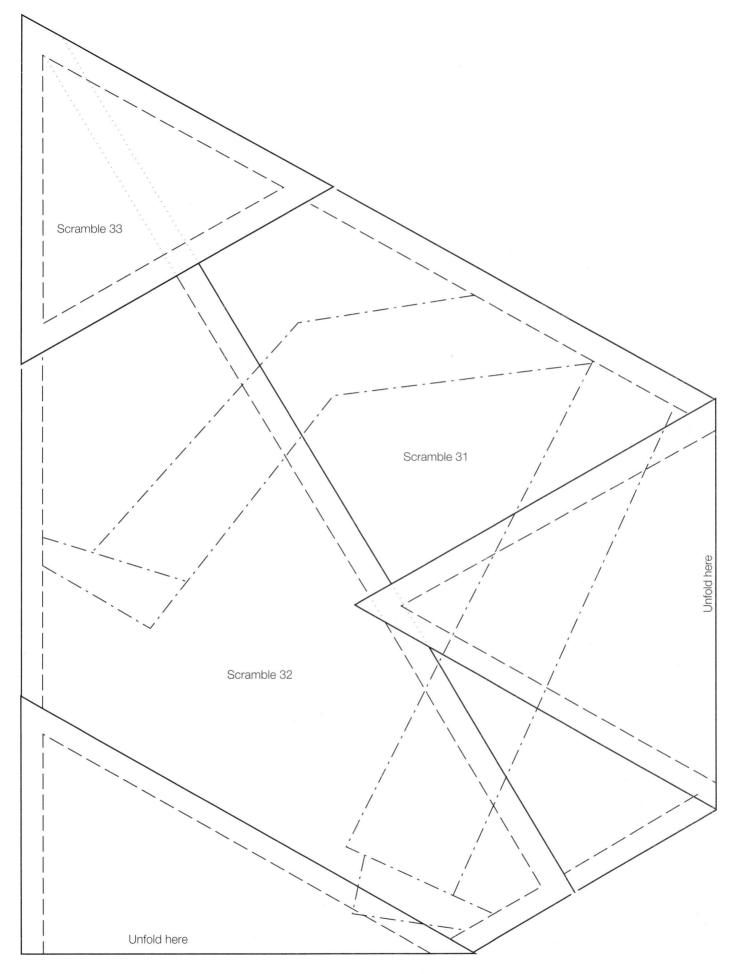

Scramble 33

Scramble 31

Scramble 32

Unfold here

Unfold here

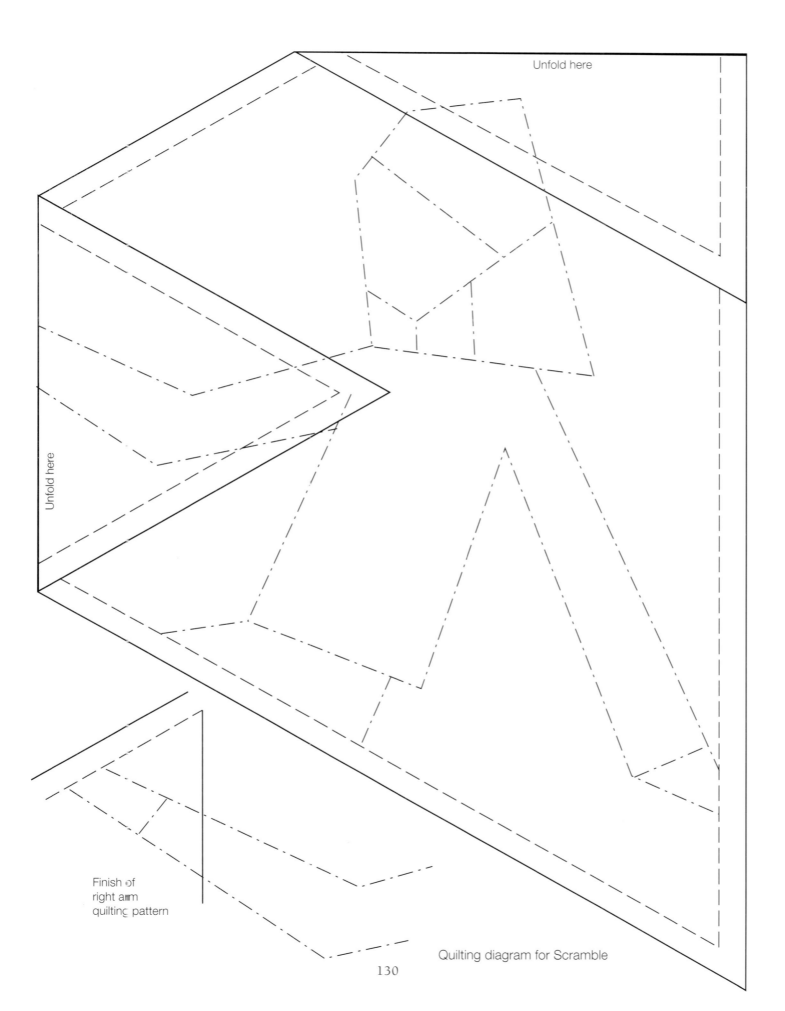

Unfold here

Unfold here

Finish of
right arm
quilting pattern

Quilting diagram for Scramble

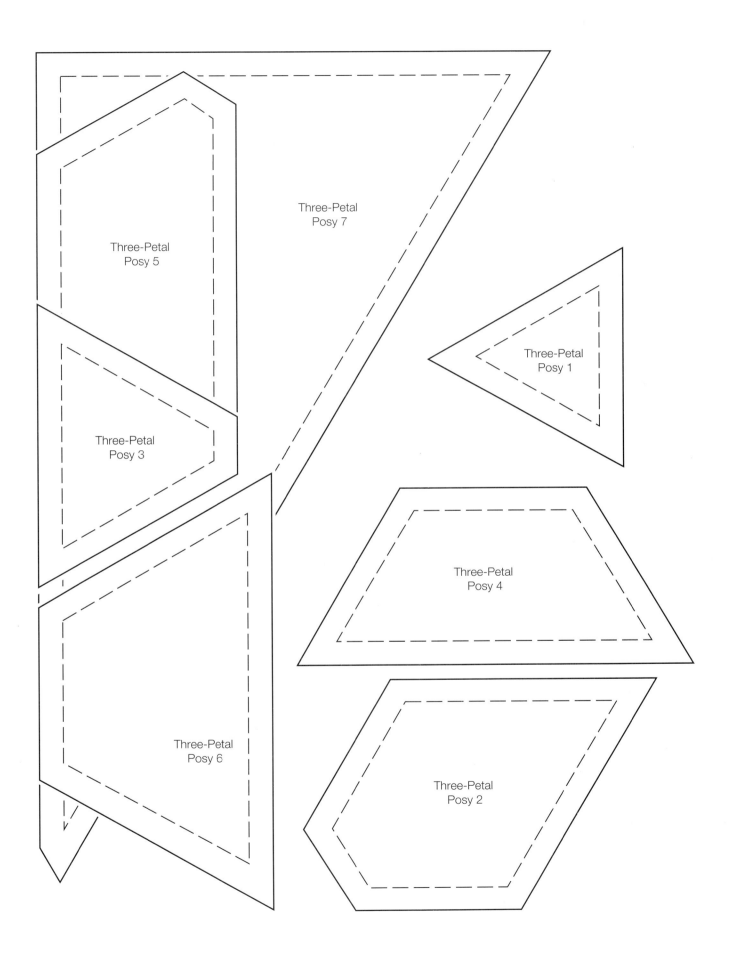

Three-Petal
Posy 7

Three-Petal
Posy 5

Three-Petal
Posy 1

Three-Petal
Posy 3

Three-Petal
Posy 4

Three-Petal
Posy 6

Three-Petal
Posy 2

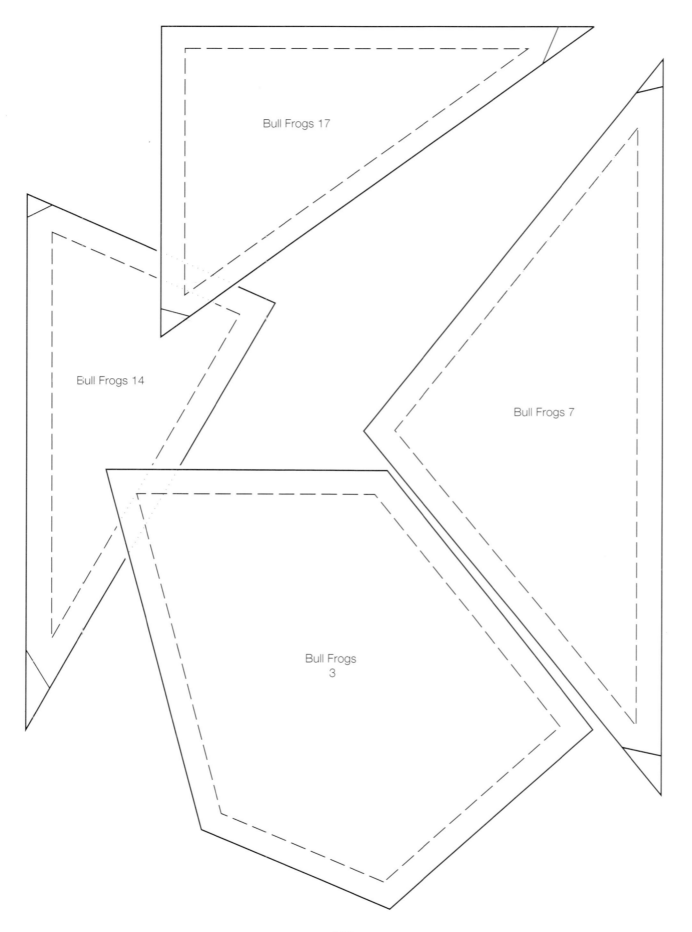

Bull Frogs 17

Bull Frogs 14

Bull Frogs 7

Bull Frogs
3

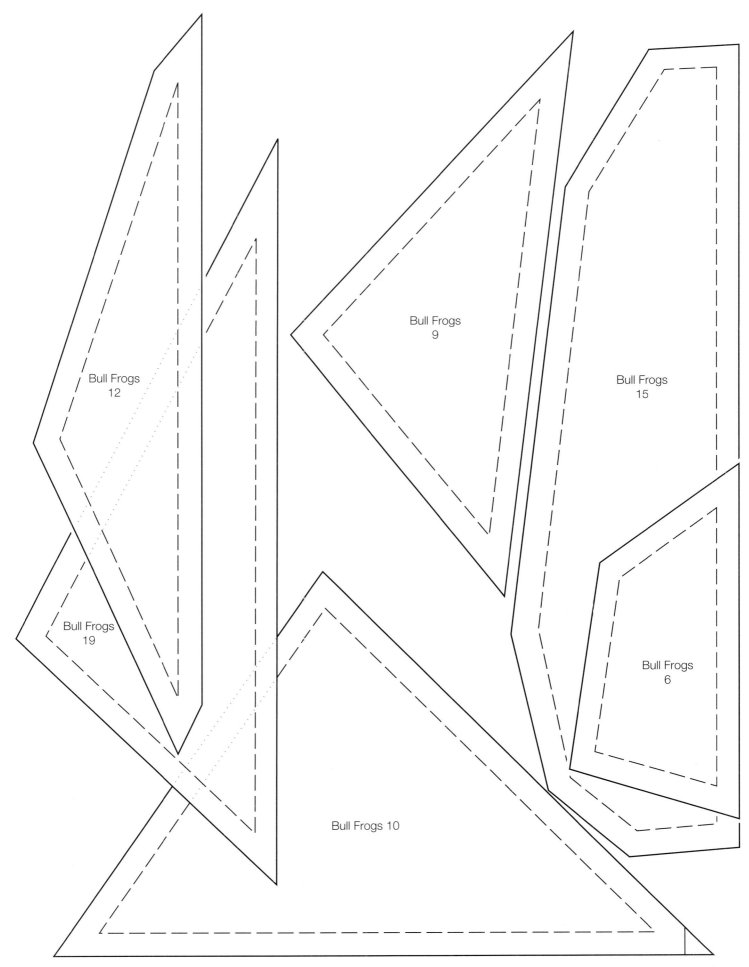

Bull Frogs
12

Bull Frogs
9

Bull Frogs
15

Bull Frogs
19

Bull Frogs
6

Bull Frogs 10

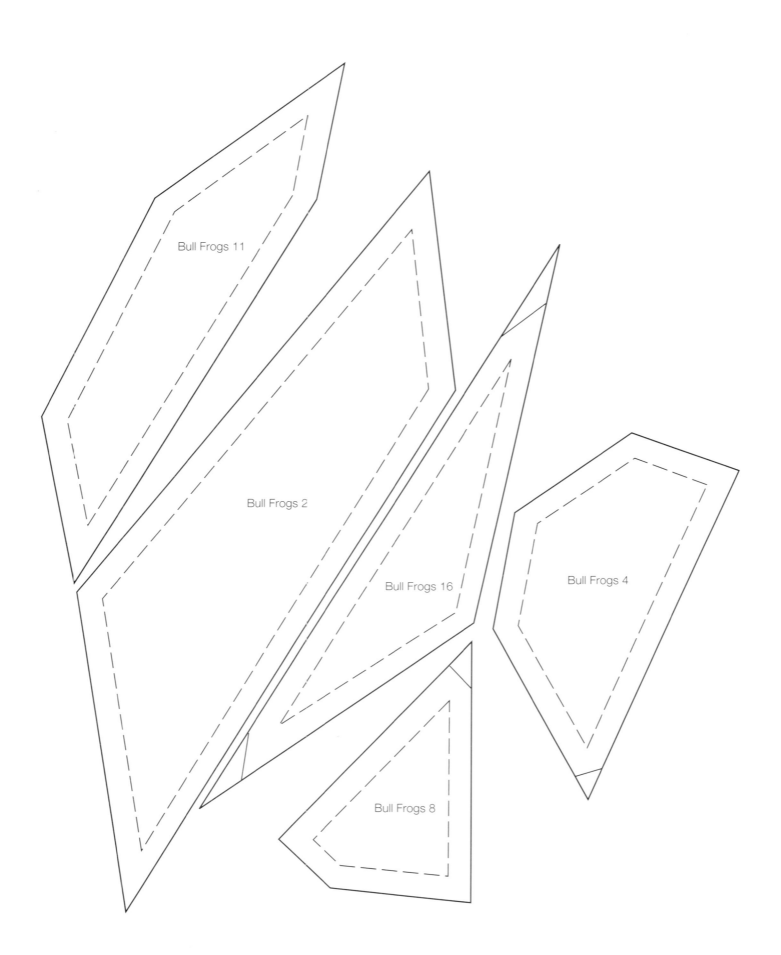

Bull Frogs 11

Bull Frogs 2

Bull Frogs 16

Bull Frogs 4

Bull Frogs 8

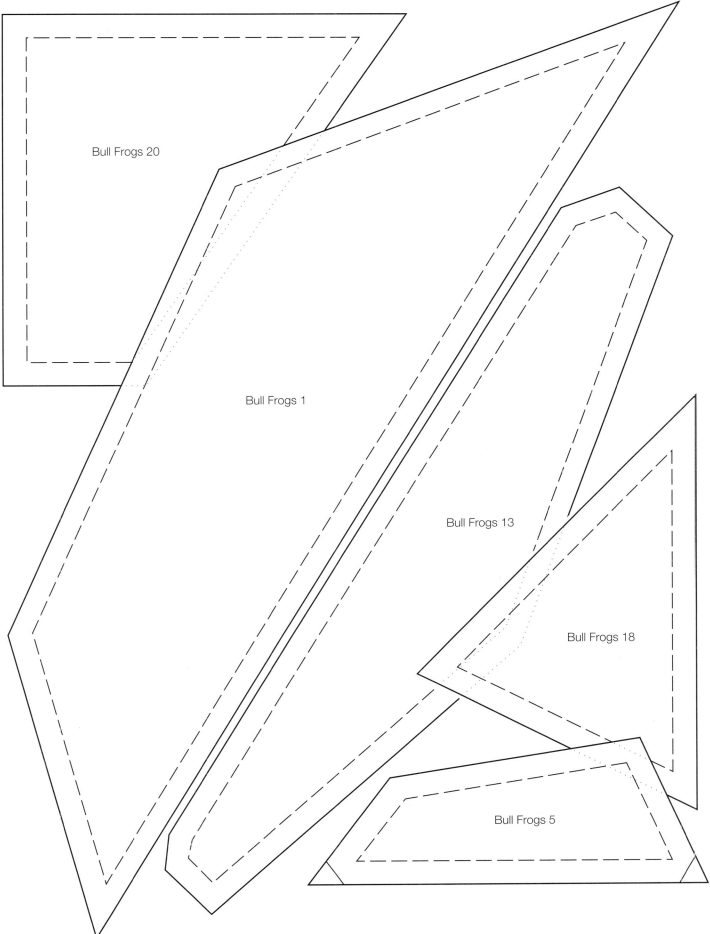

Bull Frogs 20

Bull Frogs 1

Bull Frogs 13

Bull Frogs 18

Bull Frogs 5

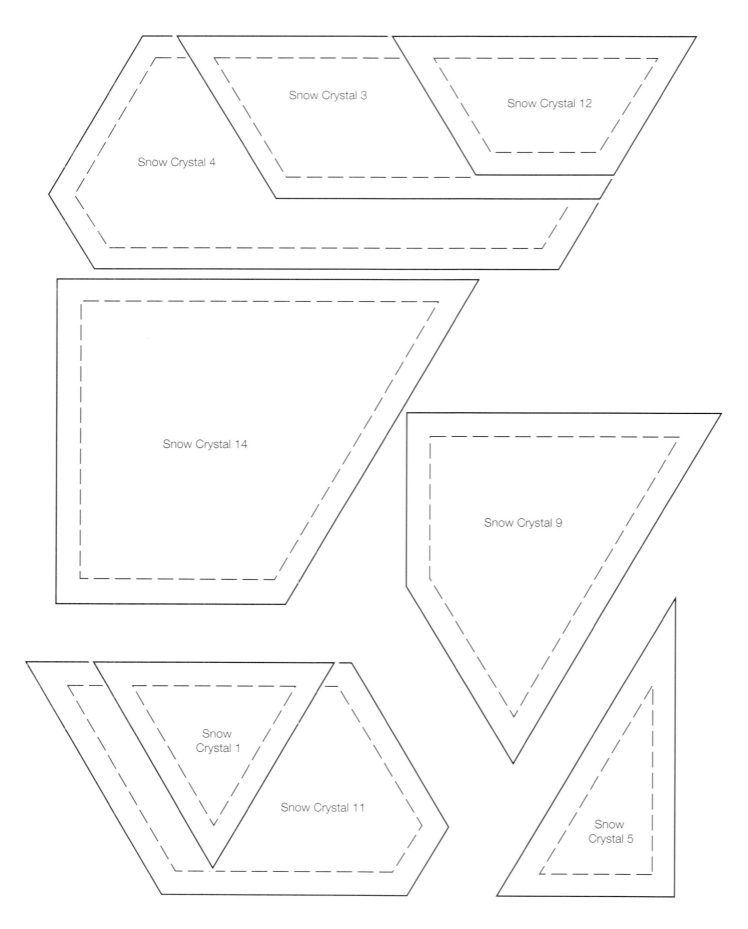

Snow Crystal 3

Snow Crystal 12

Snow Crystal 4

Snow Crystal 14

Snow Crystal 9

Snow Crystal 1

Snow Crystal 11

Snow Crystal 5

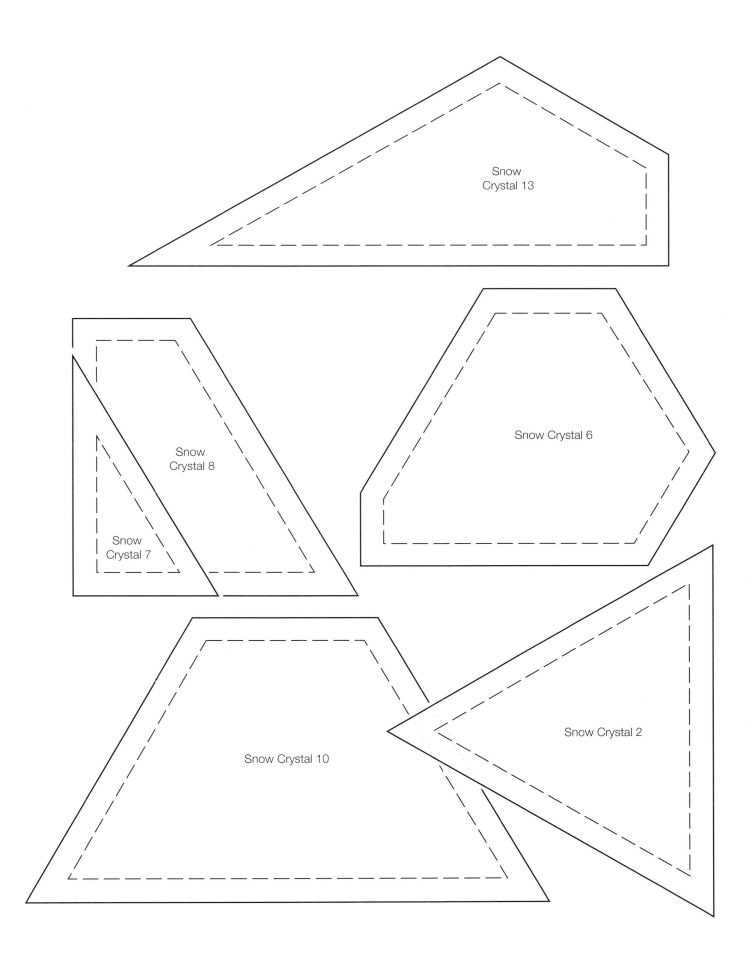

Snow
Crystal 13

Snow
Crystal 8

Snow Crystal 6

Snow
Crystal 7

Snow Crystal 10

Snow Crystal 2

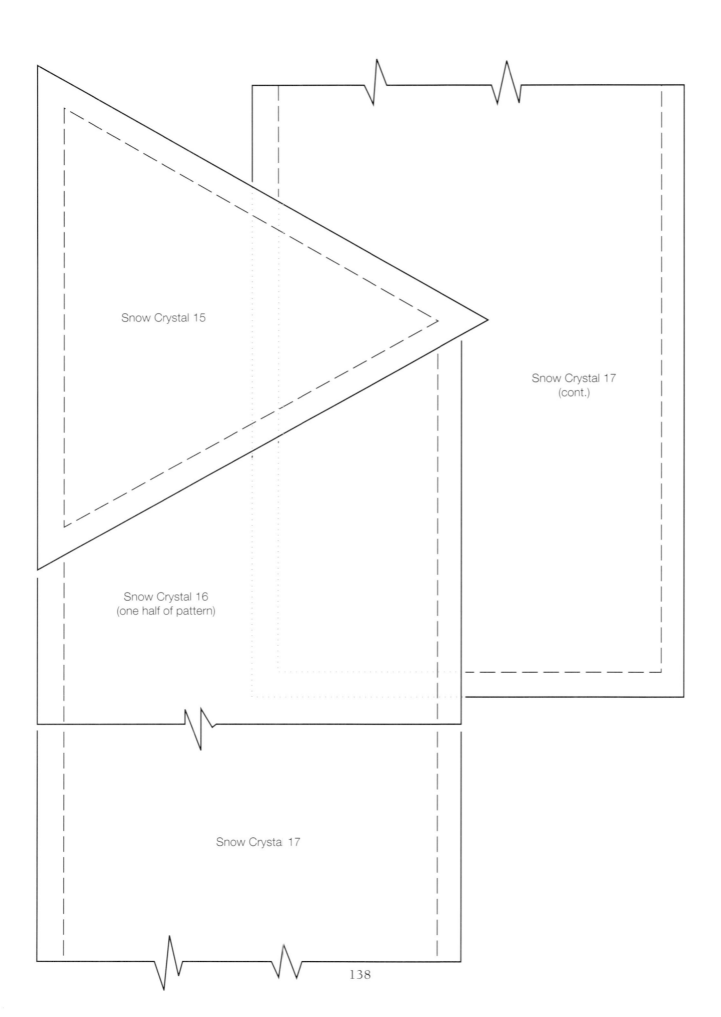

Snow Crystal 15

Snow Crystal 17
(cont.)

Snow Crystal 16
(one half of pattern)

Snow Crystal 17

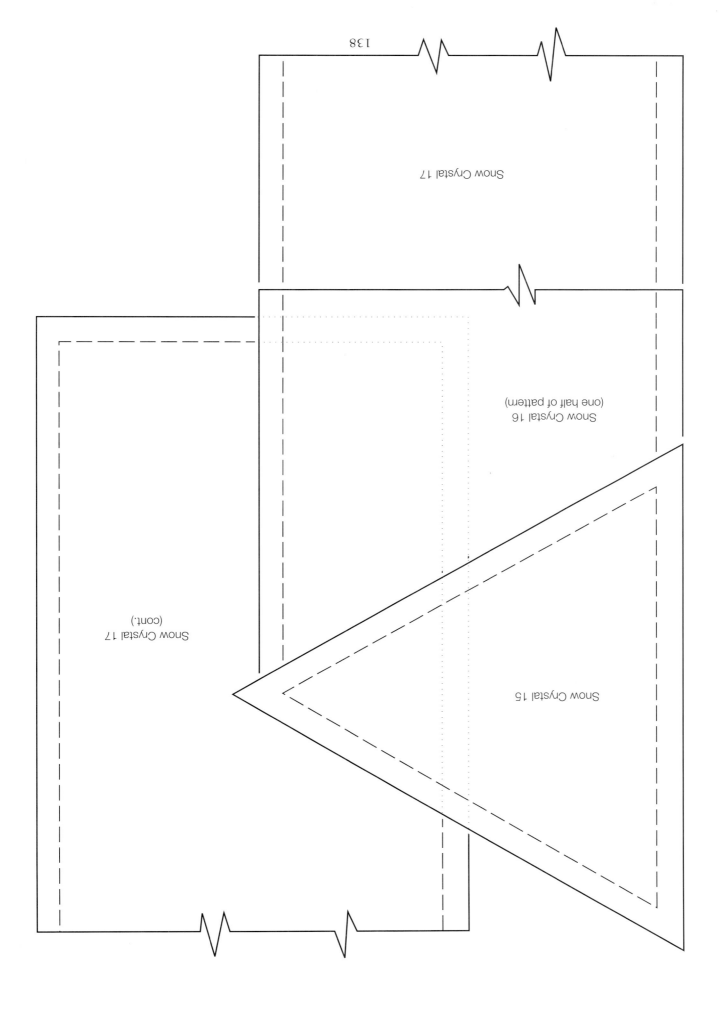

Snow Crystal 17

Snow Crystal 16
(one half of pattern)

Snow Crystal 15

Snow Crystal 17
(cont.)

138

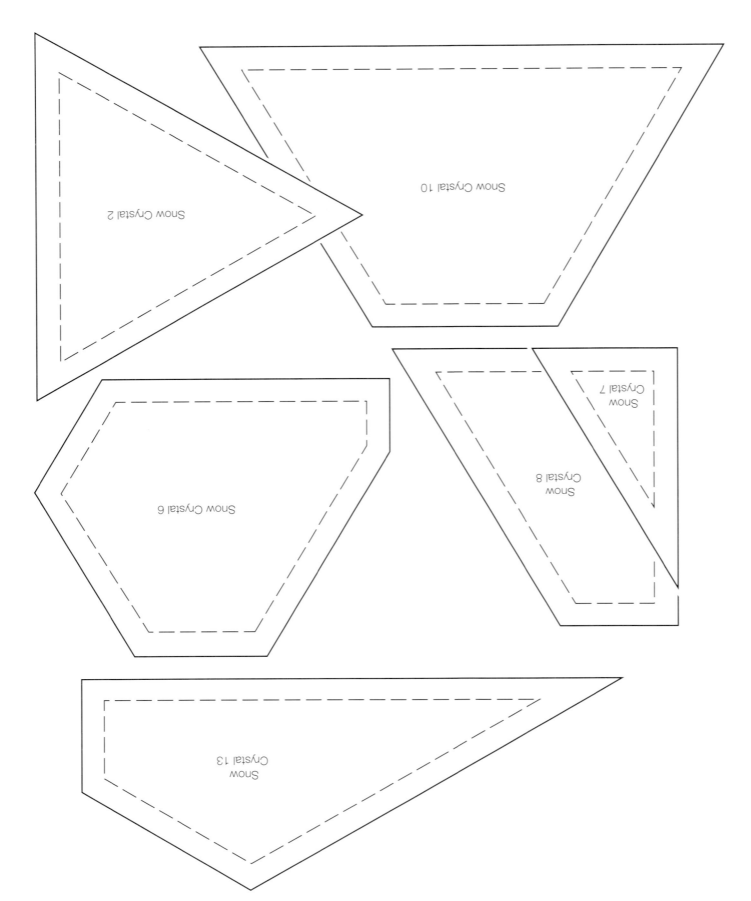

Snow Crystal 2

Snow Crystal 10

Snow Crystal 6

Snow Crystal 8

Snow Crystal 7

Snow Crystal 13

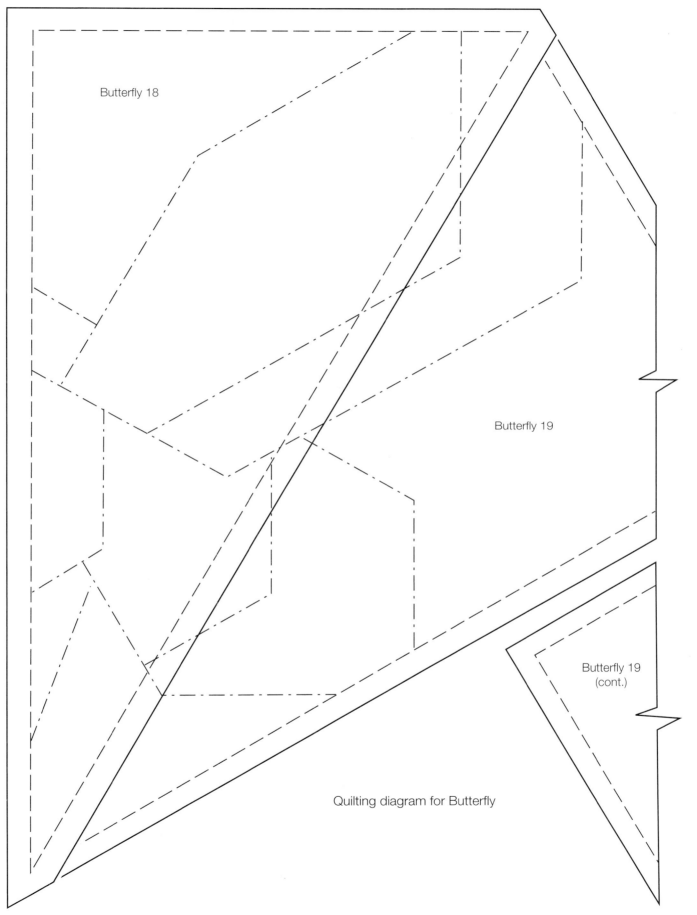

Butterfly 18

Butterfly 19

Butterfly 19
(cont.)

Quilting diagram for Butterfly

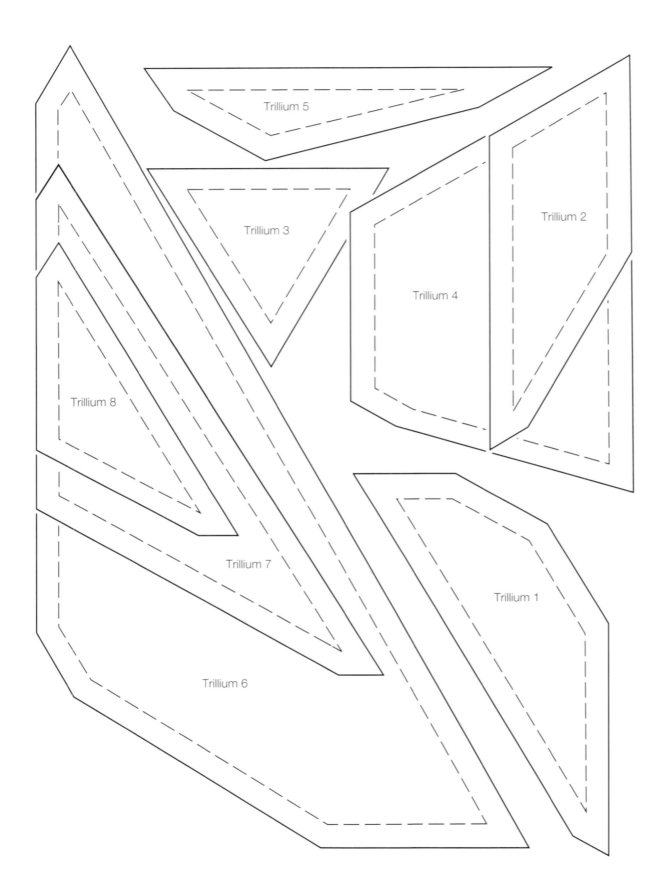

Trillium 5

Trillium 2

Trillium 3

Trillium 4

Trillium 8

Trillium 7

Trillium 1

Trillium 6

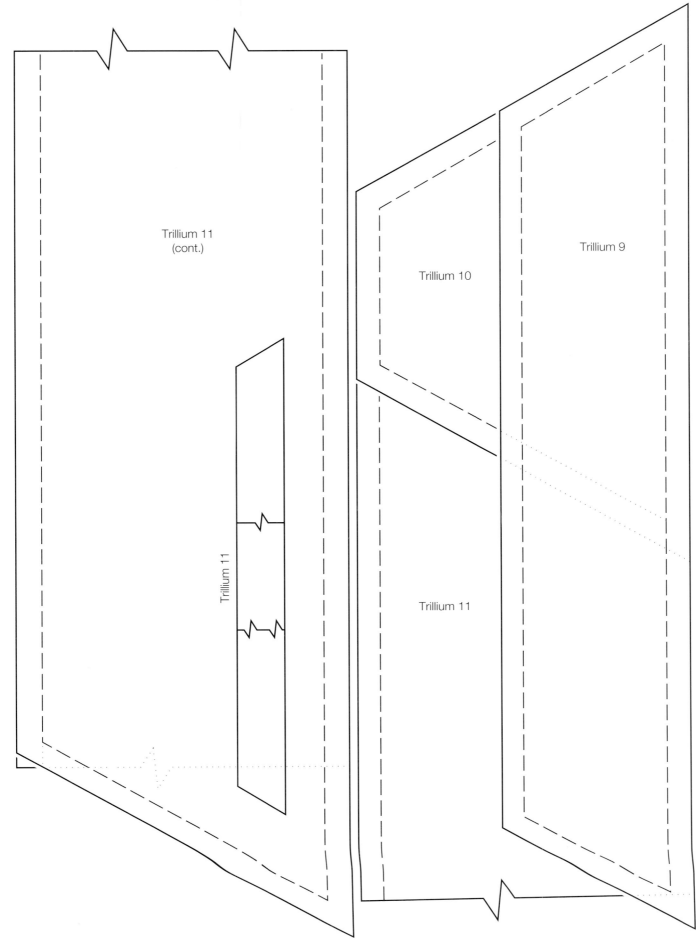

Trillium 11
(cont.)

Trillium 11

Trillium 10

Trillium 9

Trillium 11

ABOUT THE AUTHOR

Ruth B. McDowell is a full-time professional quilt artist who has taught and lectured nationally as well as in Europe, Asia, and New Zealand. In the two decades since she began her quiltmaking career, she has made over 250 quilts. Her quilts have been seen in solo shows on both coasts and in Japan, and in many invitational exhibitions; they have also been seen in dozens of magazines and books internationally.

Ruth came to quiltmaking after earning a degree in Art and Design from the Massachusetts Institute of Technology and working as an illustrator. Having begun with traditional bed quilts, she encountered the world of contemporary quilting in 1978, when she was inspired by the works of Nancy Halpern and Rhoda Cohen. From that time, she developed her own styles and techniques, building upon her interests in mathematics, gardening, and needlework. In 1991 she published her first book, *Pattern on Pattern*. With *Symmetry*, she explores concepts of block design which are readily accessible to beginners and which will inspire and delight experienced artists.

Other Fine Quilting Books From C & T Publishing

An Amish Adventure, Roberta Horton

Appliqué 12 Easy Ways! Elly Sienkiewicz

Appliqué 12 Borders and Medallions!, Elly Sienkiewicz

The Art of Silk Ribbon Embroidery, Judith Montano

Baltimore Album Quilts, Historic Notes and Antique Patterns, Elly Sienkiewicz

Baltimore Album Revival! Historic Quilts in the Making. The Catalog of C&T Publishing's Quilt Show and Contest, Elly Sienkiewicz

Baltimore Beauties and Beyond (2 Volumes), Elly Sienkiewicz

Calico and Beyond, Roberta Horton

Christmas Traditions From the Heart, Margaret Peters

Christmas Traditions From the Heart, Volume Two, Margaret Peters

A Colorful Book, Yvonne Porcella

Crazy Quilt Handbook, Judith Montano

Crazy Quilt Odyssey, Judith Montano

Design a Baltimore Album Quilt! Elly Sienkiewicz

Dimensional Appliqué—Baskets, Blooms & Borders, Elly Sienkiewicz

Fantastic Figures: Ideas & Techniques Using the New Clays, Susanna Oroyan

14,287 Pieces of Fabrics and Other Poems, Jean Ray Laury

Happy Trails, Pepper Cory

Heirloom Machine Quilting, Harriet Hargrave

Imagery on Fabric, Jean Ray Laury

Isometric Perspective, Katie Pasquini-Masopust

Landscapes & Illusions, Joen Wolfrom

The Magical Effects of Color, Joen Wolfrom

Mariner's Compass, Judy Mathieson

Mastering Machine Appliqué, Harriet Hargrave

Memorabilia Quilting, Jean Wells

The New Lone Star Handbook, Blanche Young and Helen Young Frost

Pattern Play, Doreen Speckmann

Pieced Clothing, Yvonne Porcella

Pieced Clothing Variations, Yvonne Porcella

Plaids and Stripes, Roberta Horton

Quilts, Quilts, and More Quilts! Diana McClun and Laura Nownes

Stitching Free: Easy Machine Pictures, Shirley Nilsson

Story Quilts, Mary Mashuta

3 Dimensional Design, Katie Pasquini

A Treasury of Quilt Labels, Susan McKelvey

Visions: The Art of the Quilt, Quilt San Diego

For more information write for a free catalog from

C & T Publishing
P.O. Box 1456
Lafayette, CA 94549
(1-800-284-1114)